A Cast for a Crown

A

CAST FOR A CROWN.

A Dramatic Story.

BY

HARRY CHILD.

"I have set my life upon a cast,
And I will stand the hazard of the die."
RICHARD III.

IN THREE VOLUMES.

VOL. III.

LONDON:
RICHARD BENTLEY, NEW BURLINGTON STREET.
1870.

A CAST FOR A CROWN.

CHAPTER I.

" Camillo. Pray you now observe your nephew."
THE GUARDIAN.

RALPH, during the delightful walk with
Isabelle in the wilderness, failed to
remember that many of the paths were
visible from some of the windows of the
Hall. This was especially the case in win-
ter time, when the trees were leafless and
bare. Lady Rebecca had, to her astonishment and dismay, seen the two lovers walking closely side by side. Their manner and
actions, even at that distance, could not be

VOL. III. 1

misinterpreted. She mentioned the subject to the earl, who listened gravely to her statement.

"Now what must be done?" asked Lady Rebecca, triumphantly, for, notwithstanding her piety, she could not resist an inward feeling of satisfaction in finding her predictions of evil gradually maturing.

"It is unfortunate, Rebecca, I agree with you," said the earl. "See the girl Louisa this afternoon; question her, but say nothing either to Ralph or Isabelle. If we find there is anything of the kind going forward, one or other must be sent from the place."

"One or other! Is Ralph to be forbidden the home of his forefathers because there happens to be amongst us this unknown stranger? You purposed, some days ago, a journey to London, to ascertain her parentage, if possible."

"I must do so. I will set out to-morrow."

In the afternoon Lady Rebecca required the attendance of Louisa.

"Did you take your usual walk this morning?" asked her ladyship.

"Yes, my lady."

"In the wilderness?"

"Yes. Your ladyship has forbidden us to go into the wood again."

"Did you or Isabelle see any one there?"

"No one, my lady."

"Girl, have you no fear of the fire of the Evil One? Speak the truth. Did Isabelle remain with you all the time you were there?"

"Yes, my lady."

"And you did not see Sir Ralph there?"

"No, my lady."

"Then I will tell you what I saw. I saw Sir Ralph walking with this girl—walking

1—2

close beside her. I did not see you with them. Now, you have told me a lie ?"

The girl quailed before the cold iron eye of her imperious mistress.

"Tell me the truth at once, or leave this house for ever."

The girl was silent.

"Choose either alternative. One or the other. Come, speak."

"I will tell your ladyship the truth. Sir Ralph met us in the wilderness. He wished to speak with Miss Isabelle upon the subject of their imprisonment at Sir Gilbert's."

"And he did speak with her. Why did you not tell me this at first ?"

"Because he wished me not to tell you. He said your ladyship would think his conference with Miss Isabelle as arising from another motive."

"And so you preferred, girl, serving your earthly master to the One above."

"I thought, my lady, there was no harm in obeying anyone belonging to the house of Draconbury."

"Then, thinking so, why did you not obey me, and tell me the truth at first, when I asked you? Leave me. I will forgive you, this once. But remember that you require forgiveness from One much more important than me."

When Louisa left the presence of Lady Rebecca, she hastened with the dread tidings to Ralph, and told him, word for word, what had occurred. She also shortly afterwards informed Isabelle of what had happened, begging her if questioned by Lady Rebecca to relate a story consistent with her own statement.

Ralph was in great trouble. It was the first trouble of his life, and coming so quickly after his first rapture of love, he felt it acutely. Deeply thinking, and with downcast look, he wandered to the stable, where he found Stephen. He looked at the honest fellow's open brow and manly face. Between himself and Stephen there had been, from his own infancy, a strong feeling of sympathy and friendship.

"Steeve," he said, "I am in trouble."

"You need not say that, sir. There is more gloom in your face, now, sir, than I have ever seen, before. What is it, sir? You know you can trust me?"

"I know it, Steeve. I honour your friendship. I am in love."

"And I can guess whose pretty face has put you in love."

"You can?"

"It is that young lady—Miss Isabelle. Everybody loves her, sir—everyone on the grounds. I am not surprised at what you say, Sir Ralph. If ever a human creature was made out of an angel she was, and her heart is as good as her face is pretty. She would make any man happy."

"But you know, Steeve, from what I have heard from the earl and Lady Rebecca, they would object to my marrying one, about whose birth or family they knew nothing."

"I thought the earl had made out who she was, or where she came from."

"As far as I can gather he has ascertained nothing about her. And both he and Lady Rebecca have so much of that inordinate pride of blood about them, that I am afraid they will never consent to my marrying her."

"Well, as far as regards pride of blood, Master Ralph, it is not so ridiculous at all, you see. Families are families, and breeding is breeding. I, myself, should be sorry to see the old family 'scutcheon disfigured with any blur sinister; but don't you make yourself unhappy about that, Master Ralph. I am as good a judge of human flesh and blood as I am of horses; and depend upon it that

young lady, Miss Isabelle, is as high bred as
you are—every bit.   Look at her face—
look at her kind heart—look at her action,"
he continued, for having been bred in the
stable, he looked upon the human race from
a stable point of view, " her face is as beautiful as that picture in the picture gallery
—Hebe, I think it is called—her heart is
as pure as snow, and her action is graceful-
ness itself.   There is as much difference between her and Louisa as there is between
Tito, our best carriage horse, and little
Tricksy, the tough little mule that Jack
drives to Dartford market every week—not
but what Louisa is a fine buxom girl in her
way, but still she ain't got the breed in
her.   Directly you first catch sight of Miss
Isabelle, you can see the mettle she's made
of.   To see her—to hear her—is to start
your thoughts dreaming about beauty and
goodness for an hour or more."

"This may be very true, Steeve, and is true,

I admit, but still if her parentage remains a mystery, how can I ever overcome the scruples of Lady Rebecca and the earl?"

"Yes, that's awkward. That requires a little reflection, Master Ralph. It is diffi- cult, you see, to make people believe as you believe."

"And from what I can hear there is talk of sending her or me away. Lady Rebecca saw us, it seems, this morning, in the wil- derness."

"Oh, you have been in the wilderness together, then?"

"Well, you see, Steeve, what other chance could I get of speaking to her?"

"No. You are right, Master Ralph. Lady Rebecca is most remarkably strict— looks upon love and marriage as a sort of sin, no doubt."

"If they send her away I may lose sight of her altogether."

"I don't think that. If she goes away

tell her to write always to me, and I will give you the letter. Love her faithfully, and watch over her, and I am sure we shall find, before long, that she comes of a good stock."

CHAPTER II.

"Alonzo. She's gone, and I shall see that face no more."

THE REVENGE.

"I AM going to London this morning Isabelle," said the earl the next day at breakfast, "and I shall require your company. I am going upon some business that I think will please you. I am going there to endeavour to trace your father."

A few days ago such an announcement would have filled her with delight, but now she experienced a mixed feeling of joy and sorrow; joy, because she might soon behold her father, and sorrow because she would leave Ralph.

Ralph looked up quickly, glanced at Isabelle, and notwithstanding all his efforts to the contrary, could not avoid betraying emotion. Lady Rebecca did not fail to notice his discomposure.

A little while afterwards the earl retired to his library; Lady Rebecca went to her private room; Isabelle, with the assistance of Louisa, began to prepare for her journey; and Ralph walked moodily into the stables, his face tinged with sadness and melancholy. He was just feeling the effect of the shade of the first cloud that had crossed his hitherto sunny path of life.

" What is the matter, Master Ralph ?" asked Stephen.

" She is going, and I may never see her again. The earl is going to take her to London somewhere. That confounded lynx-eyed aunt of mine has seen it all. She knows everything."

" Let me saddle your cob, Master Ralph,

and you ride with them. You can make some excuse for going."

"You can saddle the cob, Stephen, but I have got to go another road. The earl wishes me to go to Maidstone for him. Of course it's done purposely. I cannot with decency refuse to go."

"Well, there is one consolation, I shall drive the coach, Master Ralph, and I can tell you where I set them down. The coach is ordered for London. The earl is going on horseback. At least, his horse is ordered."

" I must see her somehow or other before she goes," said Ralph, "and ask her to write to me, addressing it to you. Louisa is going with her, I hear."

"Look there, Sir Ralph, they are both going into the wilderness. By heaven! they have given the old cat—beg your pardon, Sir Ralph, I did not mean to call your aunt——"

"Call her what you like, Steeve. My feelings towards her at this moment are not very amiable. I will follow them into the wilderness."

"Keep in the myrtle path, you can't be seen from the house then."

Ralph soon reached the wilderness, and, guided by the sound of footsteps, he rapidly threaded the intricate paths until he suddenly espied Isabelle and her attendant maid pacing slowly backwards and forwards. Louisa, directly she saw Ralph, left her own companion and walked a little way aside.

Isabelle was still bashful, and had not the courage to meet her lover's ardent gaze.

"Oh, Isabelle, Isabelle, this is terrible," said Ralph, seizing her hand and pressing it to his lips. "I shall always think of you. Promise me, Isabelle, that you will think of me sometimes. You will not forget me, will you?"

Her face had hitherto been bent towards the ground, but now she looked up, and in a voice that to him sounded like an angel's whisper, she said, " Never !"

Ralph bowed his head and kissed her little rosy lips. A thrill of joy ran through his heart when he found her sweetly-formed mouth not receiving his kiss passively, as it had done the one before, but was pouting with the earnestness of true maidenly love to meet his.

" You will never forget me, Isabelle, will you ?"

" Never."

" If you can, write, will you ?"

" Yes."

" Address your letters to Mr. Stephen Barflair, that is our coachman. Let me know soon where you are, and nothing on earth shall stop me from seeing you. Good-bye, good-bye ! A kiss—another—another—bless you ! bless you !"

Hastily turning round he walked rapidly from the spot. His emotion was so great that he dared not look back.

Isabelle, accompanied by Louisa, returned to the house.

"You have been crying," said Lady Rebecca.

"A twig struck her across the face, my lady, and that is the cause of the redness of her eyes," said Louisa.

Lady Rebecca looked searchingly at the maid, but the latter returned her gaze with unflinching steadiness.

"Surely she is old enough to speak for herself."

"I did not intend to offend your lady-ship," said Louisa, with assumed meekness. "If I have transgressed, I humbly ask your ladyship's pardon."

"The coach is waiting at the door. Go, and write to me occasionally. Let me know all that is happening. Isabelle, you remain

here for a few moments. I wish to speak
to you alone."

As soon as Louisa had disappeared Lady
Rebecca resumed—

" My child, you are about to go forth
again into the world, and may meet with
many temptations. Continually ask God
for His assistance, and open your heart to
Him night and morning. You are young
and inexperienced. The ways of the wicked
are full of deceit. Beware, my child, how
you listen to the counsel of any one. If
the earl fails in finding your father, he will
leave you with people who will take care of
you. Pray continually. Have you any
sin that now bears heavy on your soul ?"

" None, madam," said Isabelle.

" Oh, the conceit and self-sufficiency of
the children of this world ! You, so young,
so untried in the paths of righteousness, to
assume that you are sinless, and that you
can with pure untainted soul stand up

before the dazzling glory of God and say, 'I have no sin.' Know you not, child, that there are none of us without sin?"

"I have long known that, my lady," said Isabelle, demurely, "but I thought your ladyship, by asking if I had any sin pressing on my heart, meant, had I committed any great sin."

"And you think you have not? Have you not spoken with Sir Ralph?"

"Yes."

"And was it not sinful to listen so soon to the voice of the other sex?"

"I could not think it sinful, my lady, and I cannot think that any harm could befall me either temporally or spiritually, in speaking to and thanking one who acted so nobly in obtaining my deliverance," said Isabelle, with some slight sign of warmth and passion.

"Your tongue, child, is more skilful than

I thought. And is that all that passed between you and Sir Ralph ?"

" That is all, my lady."

" Did he not speak of poetry, of flowers, of the sky, of the brightness of the sun at the rising, and of its warm glow at its setting, of golden hair, of blue eyes, of ruby lips, of rosy cheeks,—did he mention any such trash, for of these things vain and foolish youth at his giddy age alone think and speak when they meet with damsels of their own age."

" We conversed chiefly of Sir Gilbert and his wicked conduct."

" The earl is calling. Go, child. You may kiss my hand."

Isabelle raised the cold, icy, motionless hand to her lips. It was like taking hold of a wax model. It seemed dead to all sensibility of touch. She then bowed reverentially and left the presence of Lady Rebecca. At the hall door the family coach was waiting.   Louisa was seated inside. Beside the coach was the earl on horseback. Taking her seat by Louisa, Isabelle gave one timid look round, faintly hoping that Ralph would be visible at one of the windows, but the coach drove off, and she failed to catch another glance of the face she loved so well.   She settled down in her seat, giving a deep sigh as she did so.

"I know what you are sighing for," said Louisa.

"Do you?" asked Isabelle mechanically, for her thoughts were still with Ralph in the wilderness.

"Hush, not so loud.   The earl or the coachman will hear.   Yes, you were sighing because you are leaving young Sir Ralph behind."

"He has the most beautiful eyes and features I ever saw," said Isabelle, with great fervour.

"We all think so of those we love."

" But apart from that I think so."

" Believe me, Miss Isabelle, what I say is correct. Lovers see those they love through glasses of their own making. Nevertheless young Sir Ralph is a fine noble fellow, and has a handsome face."

The coach made but slow progress, pitching and heaving, swaying and oscillating as one wheel after another plunged into a hole or quagmire ; for at that period, although so near the metropolis, the king's highway was little better than a beaten track, the road being nothing more than the natural surface of the ground, unimproved by any labour or skill. It was the first time Isabelle had travelled in a coach, yet the novelty of the situation could not arrest the flight of her thoughts towards another and distant object. Whether she admired the rich yellow silken lining of the coach, the highly polished panels, the gay trappings of the horses, the stately figure of the earl as he rode a

little in advance ; or whether she admired
the dense woodland, the distant landscape,
the wild wintry sky, or listened to the conversation of her companion, all objects and
topics like little rivulets of thought flowed
towards one grand centre—led up to one
dearly cherished and well beloved memory—
the memory of Ralph.

"Where do you say your father's house
is—near the Strand ?" asked the earl.

"It is on the banks of the river, my lord,
close to the water. A little way from
Buckingham stairs."

In a little while the tall spire of old St.
Paul's and the tower of St. Mary Overy
became visible in the distance. As they
approached the houses of the borough the
motion of the coach was less violent, the
road being more level, its comparatively
smooth surface proclaiming the care and
industry bestowed upon it by the citizens.
They stopped at the old Tabard, even then

looked upon with reverence by reason of Chaucer's immortal poem. The earl, who was fond of literature, rambled about the ancient rooms and antique galleries, admiring the grotesque carvings, and with his delicate fancy peopling the place again with Chaucer's motley crowd of Canterbury pilgrims. Having refreshed themselves they again started forward, and, crossing old London Bridge, soon reached the Chepe. As they approached the Strand bridge, Isabelle's heart beat quick, and her thoughts dwelt upon her father—for the first time since she had left Draconbury Hall thinking of any one but Ralph.

" This must be the turning," said the earl, looking round towards Isabellè.

" That is the turning, my lord. The house stands at the bottom of the street, on the right hand side," she exclaimed.

They reached the house, and the coach stopped. Strange were the thoughts which

flashed through her mind. The sight of
the heavy stone walls brought up vividly
before her memories of the past. As the
earl pulled the bell and she heard the
distant tinkle, she thought of her own
room—of how many times she had sat
there dreaming of the great world outside
—wondering then, whether the world she
was building up in her imagination by the
aid of old Margaret's tales, and the accounts
of the old romancists, was anything like the
real world which existed beyond the gate
of the house. Then she reflected of how
much she had seen of active life within the
last few days, yet how little happiness she
had experienced in actually mixing in the
great sea of humanity compared to that she
obtained from the dreamy sense of content-
ment and repose which she had experienced
when living within those walls which now
stood before her.

"No one seems to be here," said the earl,

again pulling the bell. "The house seems uninhabited."

"We left old Margaret there, my lord," said Isabelle.

"Who was old Margaret?" he asked.

"My father's housekeeper."

"Then she is not here now, or if she is, she must be very deaf."

At this moment a waterman came up. He looked at the gaily painted and gilded coach, at the young girls inside, and then at the earl, and then exclaimed : "There is no one lives at that house, your highness. It has been empty a long time."

"Did not one Merlin live here?"

"Yes, your honour, but he has been left some time. He was taken to the Tower, but I hear he has escaped. Of course he was not fool enough to come back to his old kennel."

"Escaped!" cried Isabelle.

"Yes, my lady. The king is very angry about it. At least, so report says."

"But where can he be?" said Isabelle with great anxiety.

The man shook his head.

"I saw him leave one morning. He came home one morning, and left very soon afterwards with an old woman with him. I was not going to inform upon him or watch him. It was no business of mine."

The earl questioned the man, but found he possessed no more information than that he had divulged. After reflecting a few moments he exclaimed: "We will call upon Lady Claire St. Hiliare. She is acquainted with many people at court. She may be able to give us more information."

The coachman, in obedience to a command from the earl, then turned his horses in the direction of Hamil House.

CHAPTER III.

"Lady Margaret. Fear not, friend Malcolm ; leave her
with me. She is safe ; unless this castle and the
rock it stands on is swallowed up by the sea."

IONA.

LADY CLAIRE ST. HILIARE, on receiving intelligence of the arrival of
the Earl of Draconbury, betrayed some
little emotion.

"Your ladyship seems disconcerted by
the visit of this nobleman," exclaimed Josephine.

"Can you be surprised, Josey ? The
Earl of Draconbury was my first love. I
loved him long before I saw poor St. Hiliare,
but I have reason to believe that the earl

never felt tenderly towards me—at least he
never by word or deed led me to suppose
that I was any more to him than any of
the other ladies at the French court."

"It was at the French court you saw
him then, my lady?"

"It was. When I first saw him he was
the noblest and handsomest man there.
Ah! I have never thought of him or heard
the name of Draconbury mentioned without
feeling a strange twinge at my breast,
Josey."

"Then your ladyship must still love
him."

"Of course I do."

"Is he married?"

"He was once married—at least so report
told us—at St. Germains. He had married
some obscure girl, wonderfully beautiful,
who died young. She was not recognised
by society, but after her death it seemed
that it came out that he had been married

to her. There was a child, a little son, but
it died a few hours after birth. Hey-day!
they are in the hall waiting my appearance,
and I am here, Josey, talking to you. I
must go welcome them."

Lady Claire received her visitors in the
grand hall of Hamil House. Her obeisance
to the earl was cold and formal. The
earl's bow was low and courteous, yet his
manner was distant.

"It confers upon me great honour to
receive a visit from the Earl of Draconbury."

"I am equally proud to be received so
kindly by Lady Claire St. Hiliare. Your
ladyship will remember it is long since we
met."

"Some years. And if I remember
rightly it was not in this country."

"Your ladyship is correct. It was in
France. I must acquaint your ladyship
with the object of my visit."

Lady Claire bowed, and requested him to be seated, at the same time making the same request to Isabelle. The earl then briefly related his meeting with Isabelle in the wood, her own account of her parentage, and also of her father, Merlin.

"Merlin!" said Lady Claire, "I know the name and the man well. He lived in the large stone house by the river-side. He was placed in the Tower, but has since escaped."

"Oh, madam, do you know where he has gone?" asked Isabelle.

"What do you mean, child?" she asked, in a cold tone. "Do you think I was accessory to his escape?"

"Pardon her speech, my lady," said the earl; "she is Merlin's daughter. Filial affection made her inconsiderate of speech."

"Merlin's daughter!" repeated Lady Claire, "why Merlin's an old man with white hair—a very, very old man."

"Yes, my lady, you are correct. He is old, but he has always been my father ever since I can remember."

" He was imprisoned by the king I have heard," said the earl.

" The king suspected him of high treason, I believe," replied Lady Claire. "I think myself he was innocent. I believe he was too much absorbed in his pursuits to think of king, country, or treason, or anything disconnected with his science."

" Your ladyship will now understand the object of my call. Knowing you had great interest at court, I thought—"

" Indeed," said Lady Claire, blushing in spite of every effort to the contrary, "I did not know that I possessed any interest at court. Rumour must favour me if it says so."

" At all events your ladyship must admit that your husband is one of the king's best beloved associates, and daily—"

"Is it possible, my lord, that you are not aware of his death?"

"Of whose death?"

"Count St. Hiliare. He has been dead some few weeks."

"Your words surprise me. I have so little intercourse with the world that I scarcely hear of anything. Allow me to offer your ladyship my most sincere sympathy."

Lady Claire bowed, and exclaimed:

"You see, my lord, my connection with the court has ceased. Even had poor St. Hiliare been alive I am afraid he could have assisted you but little, for every one is ignorant of Merlin's retreat. He escaped miraculously from the Tower, and has not since been heard of."

The earl looked towards Isabelle, who sat pale with emotion.

"Will your ladyship grant me a few words in private?" asked the earl.

"Certainly. If you will walk this way we shall be uninterrupted."

Leading the way into an ante-room, Lady Claire offered the earl a chair and closed the door.

"Your ladyship will pardon this request. I have already made you acquainted with the history of this young girl, as far as I am able. She has been staying at Draconbury Hall for the last few days. Probably you have never seen my sister."

"I have never had the pleasure, my lord."

"She is a good woman, but over-burdened with religious enthusiasm—buried in the gloom of Puritanism. She objects to Merlin's daughter staying at the Hall. To make matters less pleasant, my nephew has just returned from Paris, and we have discovered that he looks upon Isabelle with admiration, to use the tamest word. Your ladyship can imagine that it is undesirable that the two should remain in the same house.   Yet how can I act ?   I cannot turn her adrift."

"As you always were, my lord, so kind and noble-hearted.   The girl can stay here."

"I scarcely like to trespass upon you in this manner, Lady Claire."

"It is no trespass.   I first made the offer.   Believe me, I shall be only too happy to be, with yourself, instrumental in bringing her again to her father."

After some further conversation, the earl bade Lady Claire adieu, leaving Isabelle under the protection of her ladyship. Louisa remained also to attend upon Isabelle.

"I think I can divine the reason, Lady Claire, of your offering a home to Merlin's daughter," observed Josephine to her mistress, as they sat together late the same evening.

"No doubt you can, Josey," answered her ladyship.   "You see if Merlin ever reappears, my kindness to his daughter will make him my firm friend for ever. Besides, it is some advantage to have so powerful and noble a house as Draconbury under an obligation to oneself."

CHAPTER IV.

" Proteus. O, how this spring of love resembleth
The uncertain glory of an April day ;
Which now shows all the beauty of the sun,
And by and by a cloud takes all away !"
TWO GENTLEMEN OF VERONA.

THAT night, when Isabelle and Louisa retired to the sleeping chamber set apart for their use, they conversed long and earnestly upon the events of the last few hours.

" It is strange," said Isabelle, " that the earl has left us here. It seems that instead of discovering the whereabouts of my father, he was chiefly concerned in getting us away from Draconbury Hall."

" You have just guessed the real motive

of the journey, Miss Isabelle. Ralph's fondness for you was discovered by the old falcon."

" By whom ?"

" By the old falcon—I mean Lady Rebecca. She is always called the old falcon by us—and she would not let the earl rest until he had taken you away from the Hall."

The mention of Ralph's name called up on Isabelle's cheek a faint blush. She relapsed into silence, and sat gazing pensively at the floor. Her thoughts ran quickly over every scene in which Ralph had acted any part, from the moment he dashed through the broken window, at Sir Gilbert's, to the leave-taking she had that day had with him. A deep drawn sigh arose from her bosom.

" It is no use sighing," said Louisa, " that will never bring him nearer to you, miss. Sit down and write a letter at once. Here is pen and ink. In fact this room possesses every luxury. Lady Claire St. Hiliare is kind, very kind, in giving us such a large and well-furnished room to sleep in."

Isabelle aroused herself, and taking up the pen, sat down to write. What should she say? It was a difficult task. Should she pour forth on the paper all her deep and earnest love? How should she begin?

"You have looked at and studied the paper long enough," said Louisa, playfully, "why don't you begin, miss?"

"I don't know what to say," said Isabelle.

"Tell him we are here. Tell him we are at Hamil House. I would stake my life that he will be here within a few hours after he gets the letter, and will never rest until he sees you again."

"Sees me! How, Louisa?"

"I cannot explain how. But I am sure young Sir Ralph has too much ingenuity

and courage to let stone walls stand between him and the girl he loves.   Write
the letter, and I will get it conveyed to
Stephen Barflair, the coachman.   He will
give it to young Sir Ralph."

Isabelle began the letter.

"DEAR SIR RALPH," she wrote, and at
these words she stopped for some time.
She sat gazing at the oil-lamp which sent
its feeble rays around the room.   Then she
looked at a portrait hanging on the wall
opposite, and while her eyes were mechanically and almost unconsciously tracing the
features, the folds of the dress, the ruffles,
the massive oaken frame, and everything
connected with the picture, her thoughts
were wandering about in strange confusion,
building up imaginary epistles to the youth
she loved, clothing her ideas in dainty language, yet before she had committed them
to paper becoming dissatisfied, both with
the ideas and the words.   Half an hour

passed, still "Dear Sir Ralph" were the only words upon the paper.

"If you write only three words in half an hour," said Louisa, who, divested of half her attire, sat on a chair, waiting for Isabelle to finish, "you will have done your letter about sunrise to-morrow morning."

"It is so difficult," said Isabelle.

Another long silence ensued, during which Isabelle worked away assiduously with her pen, and then exclaimed, "I have written it at last, Louisa. This is what I have said—

"DEAR SIR RALPH,

        "I and Louisa are now staying at Hamil House. The earl left us here. I presume at the time I am writing this he has safely arrived at Draconbury. I miss seeing you very much. I shall never forget our walks in the wilderness. Indeed, I may say that I am always thinking of you. I hope to soon see you again. But pray be not rash. Never again run so much risk for me as you did at Sir Gilbert's, for which kindness I thank you with all my soul.

" With love,

" Yours,

" ISABELLE."

" Do you think I have said too much ?" she asked.

" Too much ! I should have said twice as much, and have been more warm in my expression of love for him. I think it is too cold and sedate a letter."

" I could not say much more, Louisa."

" As you please. Cold as it is it will be sufficient to bring him here before this time to-morrow. Come, let us to bed. Give me the letter. To-morrow we must see how we can send it to Stephen."

In the morning, after breakfast, Lady Claire requested Isabelle to attend her in her private chamber. Josephine was present.

"Be seated, pray," said Lady Claire, as Isabelle entered, "make yourself happy, my child. So much of your history as I have heard from the Earl of Draconbury seems quite romantic. Now tell me all about your father, and your adventures since he was placed in the Tower."

Lady Claire sat some time listening to the account of her youthful visitor. The day passed away in pleasant gossip. Isabelle had much to relate, and Lady Claire experienced a great pleasure in relating her own history, or such part as she thought fit to divulge, paying little regard to the truth of her statements, so that the narration thereof exhibited her importance, high birth, wealth, and power of beauty.

In the evening, at dusk, they were still sitting in Lady Claire's private room, partaking of the newly-introduced China drink.

A servant entered, exclaiming, " My lady, a strange man has called. He insists upon seeing your ladyship."

" Insists upon seeing me! Insists! Forsooth !"

" Yes, my lady, that is the word he used. He says he is possessed of a secret greatly affecting the welfare of all connected with the late Count St. Hiliare."

" Who is he ? What is he like ? What does he want ? Where does he come from ?"

" He is a black foreigner, my lady, and—"

The girl said no more, but screamed aloud with fright, for the hand of the stranger grasped her shoulder. He had followed her upstairs, and rudely pushed past her into the room.

Lady Claire darted a keen look of scrutiny at the stranger. His hair, moustache, and beard were white. His face was a deep dark, copper colour—almost black—yet his features betrayed none of those peculiarities common to the Ethiopian or Mongolian races. On the contrary, his features were well formed, and of the Caucasian type. The massive folds of a crimson silk turban decorated with gold filigree, and sparkling with diamonds, encircled his head. He wore a long robe of blue silk, embroidered with gold. On the shoulders and about the breast were diamonds and pearls, casting back the rays of the light in glittering and dazzling lustre. His trousers and shoes, too, were of the Eastern style. On each instep was fastened a buckle, studded with precious stones. Isabelle and Josephine gazed at the stranger with delight, wonder, and awe, while Lady Claire's brain was rapidly diving into memories of the past, endeavouring to remember whether she had ever seen or heard of such a being before.

"I must apologise for my rudeness, but

my business is important," said the stranger, bowing low and speaking in broken English. " When known it may excuse this boldness."

"I have not the pleasure of knowing to whom I am speaking," said Lady Claire.

The stranger cast a cursory glance at Josephine. He then looked at Isabelle. It was evident by the expression of his eyes that her youth, freshness, and beauty, filled him with admiration. His gaze was so long and ardent that Isabelle blushed and turned her face aside.

" When your ladyship is alone I can be more explicit," he exclaimed.

Lady Claire understood his meaning, and requested Josephine and Isabelle to retire.

" Now we are alone," said the lady, " probably I may be favoured with the object of this visit, and also who it is that now speaks to me."

" One you have never seen before."

" I believe that."

"But Count St. Hiliare I knew well—knew when he was scarce able to pronounce his own name—knew when he was a stripling — knew when he was about to be married to the handsomest woman at St. Germains ; yes, my lady, I affirm that."

"Indeed, sir, you flatter. Proceed."

"The count is dead.   Shortly before his death I received a letter in which he spoke of his passionate love towards you, and the belief that his end was approaching. He spoke of you as a child, wayward, but kind, affectionate, and loving ; easily led aside by the flattery of a crafty tongue. He deplored your being left in this country. You are ill, madam.   Shall I stop ?"

"No, no, proceed. Tell me all. It is only a momentary weakness. Poor St. Hiliare ! He was good, and kind, and noble."

"He bid me come to England, see you, and remind you of his request to leave this me."

"Where is the letter? Let me see it. I believe all you say, but I should like to see the very words he used to express his love for me."

"The letter is in this city, but it is not with me here. You shall see it the next time I see you, if you will grant me the favour of another interview. To return to its contents : he bid me warn you of one—one who is mighty in power, but weak in all that is good."

"Who ?"

"The king."

"Impossible ! The king is too generous and noble to injure or oppress a woman."

"You love him."

"Love him ! Is there harm in loving one's sovereign ?"

"Aye, but you love him not merely as a loyal subject, but as a wife should only love her husband."

"And who is to upbraid me for that? Poor St. Hiliare is dead. Am I not entitled to love whom I choose?"

"The king is already married."

"Alas, that is too true! Too well I know that! If he were not—if I could be his bondslave and knew that he loved no other, I should be happy."

"But does the king love you?"

"He did once. Ah! the sun has never shone, the birds have never warbled so sweetly, since he has been displeased with me. I have not seen him for days—earth and sky have ceased to be beautiful or have any charm for me. All—since I have lost his love—all—past, present, and future—is shrouded in deep, dark gloom. Nay—not all the past, for those memories which recall his face, his voice, his kindness, his love, are the only rays of joy that now or ever will reach my soul."

"But he does not love you. He mistrusts you. Has he not accused you of a terrible crime ?"

" I will not submit to this interrogation," said Lady Claire, rising with dignity and walking towards a small hand-bell, which stood on the table. " All this may be some trick. Show me St. Hiliare's letter and I will listen further to you, but even then I will not submit to be upbraided by a stranger. For the present our interview is ended."

" Stay, lady," said the stranger, quickly placing himself between her and the table. " Stay. I do not wish to be interrupted."

" What ! what is this ! Threatened in my own house !"

" Listen. Is it not true that the king not only accused you of a crime, but did he not suspect you of attempting to destroy his own life—to destroy it by poison ?"

" You are creating fables. You know nothing of myself nor of the king."

" I know of that which concerns the king as well as he knows himself, and of you, Lady Claire St. Hiliare, I know much. Why not leave the country ?   Can you love the king after his cruelty ?"

" He was never cruel," said Lady Claire, passionately.

" Can you love the king after the last interview you had with him ? Do you remember his coldness to you at a hut—called—Percy's Hut ?"

" How do you know all this ?   How long have you been in England ?"

" Can you love the king after that last interview ?"

" Why should I not ?"

" Then you still love him ?"

" And always shall.   Can I ever forget his face—his voice ?   Oh, that I could once more see him—that I could once more hear—"

" You shall, Claire," said the stranger in

a totally different and more natural voice. Plucking off the turban and false beard, and dropping the robe from his shoulders, the king himself stood before her.

"Charles!" exclaimed Lady Claire with joyful surprise.

"Yes, it is your truant Charles. But look at the trouble I have taken," said the king, in his old light-hearted, humorous manner, as he placed his arm round her waist and kissed her forehead. "Stained my face, and been playing the merry-andrew before you. I think it is the most serious piece of business I have performed for some time. But I am well repaid, Claire. I have found that you still love me."

"Was all this disguise necessary to dis cover that? Your majesty has too keen an insight into character to render all this necessary."

"But my long absence. Can you forgive that?"

4—2

"How many times have I told you, dear Charles, I can forgive everything?"

"Bless you, Claire! A kiss, darling. Who was that little lady I saw with you when I entered?"

"My dressing-woman, Josephine."

"No, no. I have seen her before. I know her. I mean the younger one."

"Oh!" said Lady Claire, colouring slightly, for jealousy swiftly stole into her heart, "that was a poor child—a friendless orphan. I was seeing what I could do for her."

"Whether poor, friendless, or not, her features were peculiarly interesting and striking."

"Does your majesty think so?"

"Nay, Claire, look not so troubled. That frown—those pouting lips—can I not express an opinion as to any one's features without making you jealous?"

CHAPTER V.

"Was it the work of Nature or of Art,
Which tempred so the feature of her face,
That pride and meeknesse, mixt by equall part,
Doe both appeare t' adorne her beauties grace?
For with mild pleasance, which doth pride displace,
She to her love doth looker's eyes allure;
And with stern countenance, back again doth chase
Their looser looks that stir up lustes impure;
With such strange termes her eyes she doth inure,
That with one looke, she doth my life dismay;
And with another doth it streight recure;
Her smile me drawes; her frown me drives away.
Thus doth she traine and teach me with her lookes;
Such art of eyes I never read in bookes!"

                         AMORETTI AND EPITHALAMION.

LATER in the evening, after the king
     had left, another visitor arrived at
Hamil House. Josephine, Isabelle, and

Louisa sat together engaged in conversation. Lady Claire had retired to her private room.

"A young cavalier wishes to see her ladyship," said a servant, entering the room where Josephine, Isabelle, and Louisa were sitting.

The two latter exchanged significant glances. Isabelle blushed deeply, and became so agitated that she was obliged to drop the embroidery on which she was at work.

"Lady Claire has retired," said Josephine, rising, "but I will inform her ladyship. What is his name?"

"He has given no name."

"Then he must do so. I cannot have her ladyship disturbed by these visitors, who appear to be all strangers. That horrid black man ought never to have been admitted into the house."

"It was no fault of mine."

"I am not blaming you. However I will

tell her ladyship. She can then do as she pleases about seeing him."

"It is young Sir Ralph," whispered Louisa to Isabelle, as soon as Josephine had left the room.

"It may not be," said Isabelle.

"I will stake my life on it. What is he like?" asked Louisa of the domestic who stood in the room awaiting Josephine's return, "is he young?"

"Yes, miss."

"Has he got fierce black eyes?"

"Yes; but he looks kind and good-tempered."

"He is as kind and good as he looks. Does he speak in a quick decisive way, yet in a rich kind voice?"

"He seemed to speak sharply, miss, but not unkindly."

"It is young Sir Ralph, Miss Isabelle," said Louisa; "why not go down and see? I will say you have gone to your room."

"Louisa! how can I do such a thing? Much as I wish to see him, how can I act so unmaidenly? Besides, I cannot submit to your telling an untruth for my benefit."

"I should not be so particular and prudish if it were my case," said Louisa.

At that moment Josephine returned, exclaiming:

"Show the stranger into the great hall. Her ladyship will be there immediately."

Ralph had not long to wait, for a few moments after he had entered the hall Lady Claire appeared at another door.

Ralph bowed low, exclaiming at the same time:

"I believe I have the honour of addressing Lady Claire St. Hiliare."

Lady Claire bowed and exclaimed:

"I bear that name, sir. For myself I am in ignorance as to the name of my visitor. Be seated, pray, sir."

"I am the nephew of the Earl of Dracon-bury."

"Indeed! I am glad to see you, sir. The earl himself was here but yesterday."

"It is about his visit I wish to speak. Your ladyship is jailer. Will you permit me to see your fair prisoner? You under-stand me. I see by your eyes you under-stand me."

"Then my eyes, sir, belie my intelligence, or, rather, overrate it. I am at a loss to comprehend your meaning."

"Your ladyship's tongue now performs that act of which you have just accused your eyes. It misrepresents your intelli-gence."

"You are keen and facetious, Sir Ralph," said Lady Claire, smiling.

"Not more so than your ladyship," rejoined Ralph; "but, to speak more plainly, my uncle brought here a young lady——"

"Whom you must not see."

"Then she is here?"

"She is in my charge and keeping."

"Will your ladyship let me see her then?"

"It was to prevent your seeing her that your uncle brought her from Draconbury Hall."

"I am unfortunately aware of his preju- dice, and of my aunt's aversion."

"Her parentage is unknown. Think of your family."

Lady Claire experienced a cruel pleasure in watching the features of the youth as they were alternately disturbed by expres- sions of hope or disappointment, as the prospect of seeing Isabelle appeared pro- bable or dubious. For a long time she held him in conversation upon the subject, cruelly tantalising him.

"What would the earl say if I betrayed my trust?"

"How will he know of my visit?"

"Surely you would not hint at dissemblance and treachery?"

Ralph bit his lip and seemed deeply revolving some scheme in his busy brain. Suddenly he arose, exclaiming:

"Lady Claire, you have admitted that the lady I seek is in this house. Pardon me if what I am going to say appears rude. I am, on ordinary occasions, the last person to act contrary to a lady's wishes. I shall, without asking your permission, search this house throughout, and insist upon seeing Isabelle."

"I have twenty stout and stalwart retainers on the premises."

"That is immaterial. It does not in the least affect my resolution. I will ask you once again. Will you allow me to see this lady peaceably?"

"Sit down, Sir Ralph, sit down. I have only thwarted you to see what mettle you were made of. You inherit all the fiery fearless nature of your father. I never saw him, but I have heard much of his exploits. Your uncle I have met before."

" You consent to my seeing this lady ?"

" I do, of course. Valour should always be rewarded, Sir Ralph. I will send her to you at once. But your uncle must never know this."

" He shall know nothing from me, Lady Claire."

She arose and left the room. In a few minutes Isabelle entered alone. She stood at the door after she had closed it, seeming afraid to move farther, her face covered with a deep blush.

" Isabelle ! Isabelle !" cried Ralph, stepping quickly to her side. " Thank heaven I see you again !"

He kissed her yielding face, and led her to a seat.

" Are you sorry or pleased I have come ?" he asked.

" Pleased," she murmured, her eyes filled with tears of joy ; "very pleased."

" How cruel of the earl to take you from our place.   Oh, Isabelle, these twenty-four hours have appeared like twenty-four years, or twenty-four centuries.   Did it seem long to you ?"

" Very long," she said in the same sweet low tone.

" I can never live without you, Isabelle."

She made no answer, but he felt the little soft fingers which rested in his hand tremulously squeeze his own.

" Isabelle," he said, " do not be angry with what I am going to say. The agony I have suffered since your absence makes me more precipitous than I ought to be ; besides, the earl and my gloomy aunt may discover that I see you here.   This lady—Lady Claire—may betray us. Isabelle, you must be my wife—I cannot live without

you. Would you be happy as my little
wife, Isabelle ?"

She made no answer, but again her soft
fingers pressed his ; this time passionately
and convulsively.   Her head was bowed
down, and Ralph felt a warm tear fall upon
his hand.

"Will   you   be   happy, Isabelle ?"   he
asked, gently raising her blushing face.
He saw her cheeks bedewed with tears,
but the fond, happy look of those eyes
showed they were tears of joy. She en-
deavoured to avert her face from his gaze,
but he resolutely pressed her head upon his
bosom, and kissed her fair forehead.

"You must be mine, Isabelle—mine for
ever and ever until God separates us."

" But"——said Isabelle, faintly.   She
stopped, and said no more.

" But what ?"

" I have been thinking"——she stopped
again, and squeezed his hand.

"Been thinking what?"

"You are a gentleman and nobleman by birth. I am only an orphan, and far beneath you in family."

"What of that, darling? I love you more than I could love the highest lady in the kingdom."

"But you may not always think so."

"I shall—by heaven, I shall. As long as the sun rises in the east—as long as the tide rises and falls—as long as morning follows night, and night morning, I shall love you. I have heard from the earl all he knows of you. What is your birth to me? Isabelle, do not mention this again. Do not think of it. I shall consider it unkind if you do. Who has put such a stupid idea into your head? Louisa?"

"No—no. Louisa has been kind."

"And so your little dear goosey head created the phantom itself?"

"It was natural I should think of it."

"Then don't think of it again, dear Isabelle. With regard to what you say—that I have not known you long, that may be true; but I think I can quickly judge character, and I——"

"But the earl and Lady Rebecca?"

"The earl will know nothing of it. Lady Rebecca may if she survives him. When the earl dies I take possession of the estates, unless——" He stopped, for he remembered all he had heard of the earl's marriage at Paris. "Unless," he resumed, "he marries, which does not seem at all probable. Until his death I have sufficient private income to make us both happy in a humble way, and if he marries and leaves any heir, I shall still have the same private income."

They sat some time talking of the future. Ralph was all eagerness and impulsiveness, painting everything in the most glowing colours. Isabelle sat fondly clasping his hand, with her eyes bent on the ground;

venturing, however, now and then, to steal
a furtive glance of love at his handsome
features.

"I must leave now," said Ralph at last.
"A kiss, Isabelle—a sweet, sweet kiss.
Bless you! bless you! I will come here
again to-morrow evening, and we will then
make our plans for the future."

After bidding Lady Claire adieu and
thanking her for her kindness, he left
Hamil House.

CHAPTER VI.

"*Monsieur De Paris.* But there are some who say,
jealousy is no more to be hid than a cough."
THE GENTLEMAN DANCING MASTER.

THAT same night Lady Claire and Josephine reviewed the events of the last few hours, and speculated on the future.

"You astonish me, my lady," said Josephine, "when you say that black man was the king in disguise."

"It is true, nevertheless, Josey. He still loves me. It was Charles himself. Imagine my pride when I heard him ask if I would forgive his absence so long. Oh, Charles will always be my slave. Although he seems to do so unwittingly, he obeys my

will as surely as the tender sapling bends
before the wind."

" The queen is alive still."

" Would she were dead."

" An event is not accomplished by mere
wishing.   Actions create events."

"You are right, Josey.   I must deal
with this queen another time.   At present
I am troubled by another."

" Who is that, my lady ?"

" The king, when he first entered in his
disguise this evening, looked at us all, but
did you notice how long his eyes dwelt
upon that baby chit of a wench—this girl
that the Earl of Draconbury brought here ?"

" Aye, my lady, I did.   His eyes glowed
with admiration.   He seemed ready to de-
vour her.   He looked neither at your ladyship nor myself in anything like the same
manner."

" He loves her.   It is his nature to like
new faces."

5—2

"And to remember old ones. His return here must convince your ladyship that your expressive features have great power over him."

"I am convinced of that. But I do not like his gazing at this girl, and afterwards asking who she was."

"Did he ask that? That looks ominous. He will be more bold next time, and desire to see her."

At this moment there was a tap at the door. Josephine opened it, and saw standing outside one of the domestics with a small square paper packet in her hand.

"A messenger has just brought this for her ladyship," said the domestic. Josephine received the packet, and handed it to her mistress.

"Close the door, Josey," said her ladyship. "Whatever can this be? It is addressed 'Lady Claire St. Hiliare.'"

Cutting the twine which surrounded it,

she took off the outside wrapper of paper. A letter dropped out.

"Joy! joy!" she almost shouted; "it's from the king!"

She eagerly read the letter. Josephine watched her face as she did so, and saw the bright happiness gradually fade from her features, and give place to the succeeding expressions of gloom, vexation, and rage, and hate, just as a black cloud creeping up from the west would gradually blot out the light of the sun before the coming of the tempest.

"A pest on him!" hissed Lady Claire through her teeth, as she dashed the letter on the table.

Josephine took it up and read the words, which were in the king's own handwriting :—

"MY OWN DEAR CLAIRE,

"The enclosed bauble is for your young ward. I send it merely as just homage due from an admirer of the sex to one so young and beautiful. After what has occurred I know you must be above jealousy, and feel certain that you will not be offended by this action. Yours for ever, dear Claire, and with best love,

　　　　　　　　　　"CHARLES."

"Impudent—cool—insulting," said Josephine.

"Look, here it is," said Lady Claire, holding up a diamond necklace, her eyes rivalling the lustre of the gems themselves in brilliancy; glittering, as they did, with the fierce passion of a tigress.

Josephine looked at the gems, and as they sparkled in the light, involuntarily uttered an exclamation of admiration. For the moment womanly weakness—love of baubles—overcame her usual prudence.

"You seem delighted," exclaimed Lady

Claire, fixing her fierce eyes upon the indiscreet maid.

"I could not help, my lady, admiring the stones," said Josephine, meekly, "but they are nothing compared to your best tiara. The stones are not so large, nor so heavy, nor is it above half the size. Will your ladyship give it her?"

"Give it her! yes, the young minx! To-morrow, at daybreak, she quits this house."

"But the earl?" suggested Josephine.

"The earl!" said Lady Claire; and as she stood with the necklace held out in one hand, the other clenched and outstretched, her face flushed with rage and hate, her eyes glittering with passion, she looked like one of the furies—yet with all the demoniacal passion in her face the almost indescribable fascination of her features was not demolished, but rather increased. "The earl," she exclaimed, "and young Sir Ralph, and this wench, and all of them, may sink into the lowest depths of the devil's pit before I will allow any one to stand between me and Charles, or even rob me of one glance of his eye."

"Your ladyship determines rightly. It will be easy to say that she and her maid went out for a walk and did not return."

CHAPTER VII.

" *Macbeth.*   Hence, horrible shadow !
Unreal mockery, hence !"

MACBETH.

THAT same night Carlo sat alone in the great kitchen of Hamil House. All the other servants had retired to rest. He sat in front of the fire, stretching his long legs out before it, and basking in the warm glow of the blazing logs. From the cigarrito in his mouth, he now and then lazily puffed a cloud of smoke.

Just as he was thinking of going to bed himself, the gate bell, which hung in the kitchen, gave one solitary sound, as though some one were feebly and timidly pulling the handle at the gate.

"That is strange," said the Spaniard, looking up at the bell, as it was still feebly oscillating ; "whoever can want to come in at this time of night ?"

He withdrew his eyes from the bell, and looked again at the glowing and blazing logs of the fire. He seemed little disposed to move from his comfortable berth.

"It cannot be any one wanting to come in," he muttered. "We are never quiet now. First come those two girls with the Earl of Something, then comes that Moorish-looking fellow, and then—"

A more determined pull at the bell stopped his soliloquy. Cursing the bell, and the being who pulled it, he reluctantly aroused himself, took down a lantern, and sallied forth to see who had so disturbed his peace. He pulled aside the little trap over the iron grating, and looked through the gate. He could see no one; but beneath the grating he just caught sight of a feather, and the crown of a hat. Whoever it was they were exceedingly low in stature.

"Who is it?" growled the Spaniard.

"Oh, Carlo, are you alive still? Let me in."

The Spaniard thought he had heard the voice before, but could not at that moment remember any individual to whom it might belong. Unbolting the gate, he cautiously opened it, holding the lantern so that its full light would fall upon the stranger. An ugly, deformed dwarf quickly pushed through. Casting one look at the intruder, the Spaniard uttered a cry of horror, and rushed from the spot. The dwarf followed so nimbly and quickly, that by the time Carlo had reached the house, he was close upon his heels, and prevented the Spaniard shutting the door upon him.

"Begone, foul fiend!" shrieked Carlo, his voice trembling with terror, "I did not do it. I did not drown you."

"Do not be frightened, my friend," said Zermat. "I know it was an accident, but by a miracle, almost, I escaped."

"Escaped!" gasped Carlo.

"Yes, I escaped being drowned. Let me in, and I will tell you all."

Leading the way into the kitchen, Carlo sat on one side of the fire, and Zermat on the other. The former still looked at the dwarf with suspicion, and not until he had shaken hands with him, did he believe that he was not a spirit come to avenge the dwarf's death.

"Escaped!" said Carlo, in well-feigned joy, "then God be praised! But tell me how. It must indeed have been a miracle, as you say."

"Well, you see," said Zermat, "when I pitched out into the water, I sank to the bottom like a bit of lead, because of the silver metal you had sewn in the skirt of my coat. I felt myself going down—down

—down, the water gurgling in my ears with a horrible rushing noise. I could not have been more than three or four seconds sinking, but it seemed ages—my brain seemed to work so fast. I am a good swimmer, but the heavy coat shackled every movement. A lucky thought struck me. I slipped both my arms from out of the sleeves of the coat. I was free. With one or two strokes upwards, I ascended to the surface. I could not see you anywhere, and believing you and the boat too had gone down to the bottom, I swam towards the nearest barge, and clambered on deck. I have been coming here every day to see Lady Claire, but I have been unable to spare the time. I never expected to see you here. How did you escape? The boat did not go right over, I suppose?"

"No. But it was a narrow squeak. When she righted again, I looked round for you, but could see nothing, and I fully believed you were at the bottom of the river—to lie there for ever, chained down by the silver. Thank God you are not."

"It was strange you did not see me. I could not have been under the surface more than twenty or five-and-twenty seconds."

"It was very dark—but thank Heaven you are here again."

"Yes, and ready and anxious to assist you with the remaining ingots of silver. I suppose you have not got rid of them."

"Oh, no," said Carlo, looking at Zermat, and wishing he was still at the bottom of the Thames, for now he had recovered from his first surprise, he began to see that the dwarf's reappearance would place him in a very awkward position. He was annoyed for two reasons. It would detract from his skill and ingenuity in removing people obnoxious to his mistress, and it was likewise extremely annoying to his own vanity to think that he had been outwitted by the miserable little wretch who sat before him.

"I must finish my job before morning," he thought, as he looked at Zermat. "He must die before the morning."

"Will you take some ale?" he said aloud, offering the dwarf a large tankard. "I am too tired, to-night, to speak of our future plans. You can stay here to-night."

"Oh, yes," said the dwarf, "I shall be happy to do so. In the morning I should very much like to see Lady Claire."

"In the morning we can chalk out future plans," said the Spaniard. "There are the remains of a venison pie, perhaps you can make that suffice for to-night."

After Zermat had made a good hearty supper Carlo suggested that they should both retire. They left the kitchen, the Spaniard leading the way. Proceeding down a dark narrow passage on the ground floor they arrived at a strong iron door, which Carlo opened.

"You can sleep here," he said, "it is not the most comfortable room in the house, but it is the safest. I think it will be better for her ladyship to know nothing of your visit at this hour."

"Perhaps not," said the dwarf. "You know her ladyship's humours and fancies better than I do. These great people must be humoured."

"I am almost ashamed to put you in this room," said Carlo, as though regretting his own want of hospitality, "there is no window or anything but the door."

"That is of no consequence. Here, I see, is a good clean bed, and I can rest very well on that till the morning."

"I will leave you the key," said the Spaniard. "You can lock the door then on the inside. Good night. I will call you betimes."

"Thank you. Good night," said the dwarf.

The door was shut, and the Spaniard heard Zermat lock it on the inside. He gave him the key to induce him to believe that he was master of his own egress. On the outside a heavy bolt was fixed to the door. This he slid slowly and silently into the hasp fixed in the door-post to receive it. He then left the spot. He walked along the corridor, and entered a kind of lumber room. Here he found a roughly fashioned portable stove. This he brought out and placed close against the door of Zermat's room. There was a projection in the centre of the wood-work of the door. This he picked with a knife until it came out. It was a wooden plug, which fitted into a little hole made through the wood. Into this hole he inserted a small piece of leathern pipe. The other end of the pipe was fastened to an iron chamber on the top of the stove. In this chamber he put some fresh charcoal, mixing it with the carbon ashes that were already there. All these arrangements and the methodical way in which he went to work suggested with horrible reality that the same process had been employed before. The fumes of the burning charcoal would enter the chamber, and, ascending, drive the colder air to the ground, where it would be gradually expelled between the bottom of the door and the flag-stones.

At this moment he heard footsteps within. There was a tap at the door.

" Is that you, Carlo ?" asked Zermat in a low whisper.

" Yes, yes. It is all right. Lie still till I call you in the morning."

" All right. Good night."

" Good night," rejoined the Spaniard. He then left the door, muttering as he retraced his steps to the kitchen : " I will have another can of ale, and another cigarrito, and by that time he will be asleep. I will then light the stove, and save him the trouble of waking again. He has tricked me enough already. I tried water first, because I did not want the trouble of carrying away his beastly ill-shaped body—but the rascal outwitted me. I will now try charcoal. I think I shall finish him this time."

CHAPTER VIII.

"*Leonora.* A slighted woman knows no bounds.'
  Vengeance is all the cordial she can have, so snatches
    at the nearest."

The Mistake.

THE Spaniard had not sat long enjoying
his tobacco and ale, and the cheery
blaze of the fire, before he heard light footsteps approaching the kitchen from the
direction of the great hall. The next
moment Josephine entered.

"I told her ladyship I thought you had
not yet gone to bed. Her ladyship wishes
to see you immediately."

"Wishes to see me," said Carlo, half
believing that Lady Claire had heard of or
seen Zermat return to the house.

"Yes. Pray don't look so scared, Carlo. It is nothing so very dreadful, I believe."

"Scared, indeed!" said the Spaniard. "I am not scared. Can't one look, without having his looks criticised? Where is the señora?"

"You are to come up to her own chamber."

Carlo laid aside his pipe, and followed Josephine. He bowed as he entered the presence of Lady Claire.

"Shut the door," she said. Then turning to Carlo, she exclaimed: "I have sent for you to perform an important task. You so deftly sent that dwarf to rest and oblivion, that I shall always be obliged to you, and ever remember the good service you have done. Carlo, could you deal with a lady as you dealt with that dwarf?"

"I could, señora."

"With a young girl—young, pretty, and charming. I know your iron heart is

soft as wax when the other sex are concerned."

"Señora, I could crush even an angel to
serve you. If a saint disturbed you,
señora, and you needed that saint's death,
these hands would shorten that saint's
life."

"I am satisfied. Carlo, to-morrow at sunrise, you must be prepared for a journey."

"I will be prepared, señora."

"I wish you to take two girls away into
the country. You must take them into
some forest and lose them. It is strange,"
she added, addressing Josephine, "that now
I should have the power of pleasing that
dwarf if he were still alive. This girl,
Isabelle, is Merlin's daughter—is the very
creature he was raving mad to marry."

"That ugly little dwarf who was drowned
by Carlo?" asked Josephine.

"Yes. I almost wish he were still alive.
He should then take this girl and deal with

her as he liked. I should then be making an eternal friend and slave of him, and avenging myself upon the little meek-faced vixen. The dwarf would not have been a bad ally. His skill in getting into the palace, his cunning and artifice, his ingenuity—all were marvellous. S'death, I am sorry, Carlo, we killed him so soon !"

" He is not killed, señora—he is not dead. He is alive, and now in this house."

" Perdition !" cried Lady Claire, her face turning pale and her eyes glittering with passion. "Deceived by you, Carlo ? You told me he was drowned. How is this, man ?"

"So I believed, señora, till to-night. An hour ago he returned. It seems, when he was at the bottom of the river, he, like an eel, slipped out of his coat which contained the supposed silver ingots, and swam to the top again. He must have the courage and skill of the devil—saving your presence, señora — to have done such a thing."

" And is he alive, and in this house ?"

" He is, señora.   To live or die—as your ladyship decrees.   Maddened by his appearance, and savage to find that I had been outwitted, and fearful lest I should for ever incur your displeasure, should you hear he was still alive, I have persuaded him to sleep in a close room.   By this time, had not your ladyship sent for me, that room would have been filled with charcoal-smoke, and the dwarf would have passed into eternity.   Shall it be done, señora, or not ?"

" No, no.   Go wake him.   Bring him here.   Bring him immediately."

" Your wish shall be obeyed.   He knows nothing of my previous attempt to destroy him--he believes that was an accident— nor of the nature of the room in which he sleeps to-night.   It will be as well, señora, that you should speak and act towards him as though you had never ordered his death."

"Go fetch him, Carlo. Your advice is well meant, but can you think me so simple that I should require from you a lesson in duplicity?"

"Pardon my impertinence."

"I pardon almost anything, Carlo, in one who serves me so faithfully as you do."

The Spaniard lost no time in making his way to the room in which he had placed the dwarf. He removed the charcoal apparatus, and shot back the ponderous bolt. Finding, however, the door locked on the inside, he kicked vigorously at the heavy oak, producing a deafening noise. He listened, but no answer was returned. Again and again he kicked, but still there was no response from within.

"The ugly little wretch must have smelt the charcoal, and have died from fright," he muttered.

Again he knocked, but still he received
no answer.

The sound of a short cough made him
look along the corridor. A chill of horror
ran through his frame. A superstitious
feeling of awe seized him, and held him
spell-bound. The blood left his face, making even his swarthy skin look pale and
ghastly. Approaching him was an object
which he saw could be no other than the
dwarf himself or his apparition. Had he
been all along dealing with a spirit ? Was
the figure he had let in at the gate, enter-
tained in the kitchen, and, finally, safely
bolted in the room, no earthly being,
but the dwarf's unhappy and revengeful
soul ?

These thoughts rushed through his mind
with fearful velocity, throwing him into a
profuse perspiration, and making him
tremble with fear ; for the Spaniard, brave
and fearless in face of any mortal foe, was a

puny, shivering child when seized by any supernatural dread.

"I must apologise for leaving my room," said the dwarf, approaching closer towards the Spaniard, who in his turn retreated, staring at the diminutive being before him as though he beheld the Evil One.

"You seem alarmed," said the dwarf.

"Alarmed!" said the Spaniard, in a hollow, tremulous voice. "Alarmed! Can I be otherwise? Are you the Devil himself."

"No, my good friend, I am a respectable living subject of his majesty King Charles the Second."

"But you were in there just now," said Carlo, pointing to the door.

"Yes; but I did not like being in there. You see I always carry with me sundry articles of usefulness; among them several pieces of string and wire. I saw a light through this hole after you had shut me in, and previously I heard the creaking of a bolt being slid across the door. Friend Carlo, if you cannot trust me how can I trust you? I put a piece of wire through the hole and luckily caught the burr on the bolt—but never mind—I will not tell you further, or you will be as clever as myself. Be satisfied in knowing that I unshot the bolt, and walked out, and locked the door after me, and put this Christian apparatus —this devil's burning pot—in its original position. How kind of you to give me this soothing vapour to send me to sleep! Did you think I appeared so sleepless that nothing less than charcoal fumes would make me slumber? Kind, hospitable man!"

"You must be Satan himself."

"Nay, friend Carlo, do not flatter me so much. I have not the power of his Dusky Majesty, or you should feel it. I am a poor human being like yourself. Why did you give me a key to lock myself in, and afterwards shoot the bolt on the outside?"

"The bolt is always shot on the outside. If I had left it undone, any one passing would suspect there was some one inside. I wished to prevent any one thinking you were in the house."

"And the charcoal pipe and pot, friend Carlo?"

"Is always outside, too, at night. It is an arrangement to warm her ladyship's sleeping chamber."

"Indeed. Then her chamber is over here."

"No. The heat from this room goes through very small pipes, and is led round her room. Charcoal you know is a great heat conductor—multiplying it a million times, pretty well."

"That is a new discovery then. My old master never dreamt of that," said the dwarf sarcastically.

"I placed the apparatus there to avoid suspicion. But, friend Zermat, her ladyship might have been frozen to death before I should have thought of lighting it while you were in there."

"Ah, then all my suspicions are groundless," said the dwarf; but a strange twinkle in his eyes seemed to belie his words. "Well, well, I am sorry I was ever led to suspect you of foul play, friend Carlo."

"I am sorry likewise. Gentlemen who have a common interest—I refer to the silver ingots—should be above suspecting each other. To show you, friend Zermat, that I was never dreaming of tricking you, I have got good news for you. I have seen the señora. I have pleaded for you as I could scarcely plead for myself. She wishes to see you immediately."

"Then I will go, friend Carlo. Forgive my momentary suspicion."

"Friend Zermat, we have each of us

too much nobility of soul to harbour revenge."

"Carlo, my friend, you are right. Give me your arm. Lead me at once to her ladyship's room."

When Zermat entered the room her ladyship bowed. The dwarf returned the salute with profound reverence.

"Your ladyship wishes to speak to me," said the dwarf.

"I do; you have not forgotten what you mentioned to me respecting Merlin's daughter?"

"No, my lady."

"Nor your promise to remain always my fast and firm friend, provided I performed a certain request you made respecting Merlin's daughter ?"

"I have not forgotten our compact, my lady."

"Then I have found Merlin's daughter. She is now in this house."

"What, Isabelle?"

" Yes; you shall see her to-morrow. I wish to get rid of her—never to see her again."

" Once place her in my power, and your ladyship shall never see her again."

"To-morrow, then, at sunrise, be ready for a journey. Have you heard anything of Merlin?"

" Nothing whatever, my lady."

" Of the king?"

" Nothing."

" In the event of necessity arising, I may rely on your assistance."

" You may, my lady. Since I first heard of Merlin's escape, he has not been near his old house. I have had some one watching for him. Believe me, the first time he ventures there he will be taken."

" Then to-morrow morning you will be ready. Call again in two days if possible. Good night."

"Good night, my lady."

Zermat retired with Carlo to the kitchen.

"This is a slice of luck," said the dwarf, with glee, "I shall ever deem her ladyship to be my greatest friend. As for you, friend Carlo, I revere your nobility of character as I do the goodness of my patron saint. I blush to think I ever mistrusted—"

"Friend Zermat, let the unhappy past be buried in oblivion."

"Carlo, my esteemed friend, it shall be so buried as you wish."

"Friend Zermat, I pledge you your life and happiness in this horn of ale."

"I drink the like to thee, friend Carlo."

"Here is to thy pure and manly soul!"

"And here is to thy good, great, just, and benevolent heart!"

The two firm friends, having such faith in each other, found little difficulty, assisted by the ale, in sketching out plans for the morning's work.

CHAPTER IX.

Mandane. (*Shows a dagger.*) "'Tis well; and in
return I give thee——This !" (*Stabs him.*)

BUSIRIS, KING OF EGYPT.

EARLY in the morning Isabelle and
Louisa were awakened by a tremendous thumping at the door.

"What is it?" asked Louisa.

"Get up immediately," answered one of
the domestics, "the earl wishes you to
return to Draconbury Hall at once."

"But it is scarcely daylight."

"Lady Claire wishes you to come down
immediately."

Isabelle and Louisa hastily dressed and
went down stairs to the great hall. Here
they found a bright fire burning, the table

spread with cold meats, cakes, and ale, and the new China drink. Lady Claire was sitting before the fire.

" You are to start immediately," said her ladyship. " The earl sent a messenger last night after you had retired to bed. Come, get some breakfast. Carlo is to go with you. You can have my coach."

Isabelle and Louisa made a hasty repast, and after bidding Lady Claire adieu, they got into the coach, and Carlo, mounting the box, drove them out of the court-yard of Hamil House.

The sun was just rising. His pale golden beams fell upon the tall graceful spire of old Saint Paul's, and upon the quaint gable ends and steep roofs of the picturesque old houses, bathing everything they touched in a flood of soft amber light. In places, the glittering rays shot through openings in the rows of the wooden houses, throwing across the street broad beams of light, and tracing

7—2

in shadow the outline of the irregular and fantastic roofs on the roadway below. The morning air was crisp and invigorating. It painted bright roses on the cheeks of the girls, increased the sparkling lustre of their eyes, and like the true elixir of life augmented the joyousness of their hearts. They were returning to Draconbury Hall. This was all Isabelle could think of. Every object she saw—the little white fleecy clouds sailing across the sky, tipped with golden light, the glittering towers and spires of the numerous churches, the quaint gables of the houses, the picturesque wooden balconies overhanging the streets, the immense grotesque signs bearing strange emblems and stranger inscriptions—all seemed mystically to connect itself with Ralph.

The coach went lumbering along, not that it was badly constructed—it was one of the best manufactured at that period, but the streets were execrable.

" Which way is he going ?" said Louisa, looking out both sides of the coach, after they had been some time progressing. "We ought to have reached the bridge before now."

" I know so little of the town," answered Isabelle, " I cannot tell."

Louisa called to the Spaniard. He sat proudly and sturdily upright on the box, his broad back towards them. He either did not hear or treated their admonitions with contempt.

"We are not going right for Draconbury Hall," said Louisa.

" Are we not ?" asked Isabelle in alarm. "Yes ; there is the wood. We are just going to enter it."

" But we ought to have crossed the river by this time. Long before this."

" We may have done so without notic- ing it."

" We could scarcely have done that."

The coach entered the wood. In another ten minutes it stopped. Carlo descended from his seat, and coming to the window, exclaimed : " Now, señora, if you want any refreshment you can have it here."

" Have it here ?" said Louisa, " with no house near ! Have you come right for Draconbury Hall ? How far are we from the Earl of Draconbury's place ?"

" About three miles."

" What wood is this ?"

" I forget the name, señora. Would you like some refreshment, señora ?"

" Where is it to come from ?"

" I have not forgotten that you might feel hungry."

He took from beneath the box of the coach a bottle of wine and a large cake.

" We have been calling for you to stop, but you took no notice of our cries. We thought you were not taking us in the right direction."

"Pardon me, señora. We shall be at the Earl of Draconbury's in about half an hour."

Isabelle and Louisa then partook of the refreshment placed before them. The keen morning air had sharpened their appetites. Carlo was particularly polite and attentive.

"Perhaps you would like a little walk?" said the Spaniard. "I shall rest the horses here for ten minutes or so."

The two girls alighted gaily from the coach. The forest was charming. The bright morning sun was calling from every little feathered songster its sweetest and fullest song. They had strolled some little distance, when Isabelle exclaimed:

"Do not let us lose our way as we did before."

"Hark! what is that?" said Louisa. "It's the rumbling of the coach! He has never gone and left us here!"

Isabelle turned pale with fright. They

hastily retraced their steps. When they arrived at the spot where they had left the coach it was nowhere to be seen. On the ground the marks of the wheels where it had turned round were plainly visible.

"We are betrayed!" said Louisa.

"Oh heaven have mercy on us!"

"Betrayed, and we know not where we are. I do not know what wood this is. Ah! I see it all now. That villain never meant to take us to Draconbury Hall. I believe we are still on the north of the river. Hark! a footstep!"

"The dwarf— Zermat!" shrieked Isabelle, clinging to Louisa for protection.

Louisa put her arm round the waist of her young companion. She looked at the creature approaching, and saw it was the same figure and face she had previously seen by her bed-side.

"Who are you?" asked Louisa.

"Ask your companion," returned the

dwarf. "She will tell you I am her betrothed husband."

"She will tell me nothing now, for see she has fainted. If you are human get some water from that little rivulet. Quick!"

Zermat ran to the brook, but when he returned Isabelle was slowly recovering. Opening her eyes and seeing his ugly features, she shuddered and shut them again.

"What wood is this?" asked Louisa.

"Epping Forest," answered the dwarf with a profound bow, which seemed partly reverential, but nevertheless somewhat ironical.

"Then we are some distance from Draconbury Hall?"

"Draconbury Hall I believe is in Kent. Epping Forest is in Essex. The river runs between the two places."

"That villainous Spaniard has deceived us, and has deceived Lady Claire also."

"Pardon me if I contradict you. Lady Claire St. Hiliare knew exactly what was going to happen and what has happened. It was partly by her orders. I had the pleasure of meeting Lady Claire St. Hiliare at Whitehall, at a feast given by his majesty the king some time ago, when she promised to use all her influence to make that young lady my wife, and—"

Louisa laughed outright notwithstanding her alarm. It was so droll, and seemed so impossible to think that Isabelle with her delicate beauty could ever become the wife of the ugly little imp before her. Isabelle, pale as death, clung closer to her protector.

"You may laugh, my girl," said the dwarf, "but it is true. I was in Hamil House last night. All that has happened this morning was preconcerted. To show you that I tell no lie I will produce this rope."

The two girls cringed closer together, yet in Louisa there was a fearless and almost defiant demeanour. She placed her right hand in her bosom, and watched with keen glittering eyes every movement of the dwarf.

"You see this rope, my lady," he continued, addressing Louisa, "that is to bind you with. You see if I take you both with me it might be inconvenient. Therefore I shall bind you to a tree. Do not be alarmed. You will be released in a little while by a very simple arrangement. You see this rope. When attached to you it will go round the tree twice. One circle of the rope will be lower than the other. On the lower circle I shall fix this taper. The wick of the taper will reach much above the higher circle of the rope, but when it has burned probably half an hour, the flame will touch the higher circle and burn it asunder. You will then be re-

leased. You see I wish to practise no
cruelty."

"I see," said Louisa, breathing quickly.
It was evident by the expression of her
features that her nerves were at the highest
tension. Her eyes, dilated with fierceness,
followed his movements as a panther would
watch the actions of a leopard.

"Now," said Zermat, "to show you that
it will be useless to resist me, I will give
you an illustration of my strength."

He jumped up from the ground with the
agility of an ape, and clinging to a big
bough of an oak, under which they stood,
he with his weight bent it to the ground. _
Then grasping it with both hands and using
his two thumbs as levers, he snapped the
tough wood in two.

"There !" he exclaimed, "now you see
it would be useless to attempt to resist me.
Allow me to bind you quietly, and I assure
you you will find your bonds fall off in half

an hour. In the mean time I shall have taken away my future wife."

He approached towards them. Isabelle shuddered, and, uttering a faint scream, cringed behind Louisa.

"You agree that I may bind you?"

"Certainly," said Louisa.

He approached closer. Suddenly the girl's hand flew up from her bosom. The dwarf saw something glitter in it. He was too late. Before he had time to spring aside, her hand descended with all the dread force hatred, rage, and fear of death could lend to her natural strength. The thin, steel blade entered the dwarf's shoulder, and he sank on the ground, uttering a low moan. Blood gushed forth from the wound, and ran about, staining with its ruby dye the dead, fallen leaves.

"You see, too, fiend, I was prepared as well," said Louisa.

"Oh! what have you done?" said Isabelle, looking down with horror upon the bleeding dwarf.

"Crushed a reptile. Come we must be off. He may recover. Oh, Heaven, which is the way out of this dreadful wood ?"

They both ran from the spot, threading their way through the bushes, and between the huge trees. Panting with the exertion they at last stopped when they had traversed some little distance.

"Oh, what shall I do with this ?" asked Louisa.

Isabelle looked. It was the dagger which she held stretched out from her, still smeared with the dwarf's blood.

"Throw it away—oh, throw it away."

"No. It is a horrid thing, but I cannot throw it away. It has done us good service—saved us from worse than death perhaps."

She stooped and wiped the blood-stained steel on the dry leaves and grass at her feet. When she had finished she looked at Isabelle, and exclaimed, "Give me that necklace. At least do not wear it. Put it out of sight—in your pocket, or somewhere. I saw that miserable dwarf look at it with eager eyes. The Spaniard, too, noticed it. No doubt they both meant to have had it."

"Do you think the earl has really sent to Lady Claire for us to return to Draconbury Hall?"

"I do not know. There is some mystery about it. Oh, this forest, it seems never-ending. Surely we shall, before night, see some cottage or human being. It will be dreadful to be here when it is dark."

"Heaven grant that we may not. Supposing that dwarf dies, Louisa."

"Don't speak of it. Come along. Let us get shelter somewhere, and then we will talk of the past, and of what is to come."

They hurried onward as fast as their

trembling limbs would allow them. Both were horrified by what had occurred. It was a terrible reflection—the thought of having taken away a life.

The rough road led deeper and deeper into the forest. The underwood became more sparse and scanty, but the grand old trees rose up on either side of the narrow track, spreading out and interlacing their branches above in such a manner that to look on either side the eye travelled beneath an immense and far-spreading canopy, the trunks of the trees looking like the pillars of a cathedral, while the boughs and smaller and higher branches appeared like the springings of the arches of the roof, and the fretwork of the ceiling.

The two girls hurried along. The bright wintry sun was throwing his golden rays on the tops of the trees, lighting them up with pale amber, piercing through the branches, and casting a shadowy tracing of their curious interlacings upon the grass beneath. The birds were singing merrily, making the wood resound with their sweet melodies. Now and then a timid hare or rabbit started up and ran a few yards from their path. Occasionally the deer left off grazing to look and wonder at the intruders. Yet with all these signs of life the forest seemed dreary and dull, and the feeling of gloom was deepened as they reflected that behind they had left a fellow-being probably making his last gasp for dear life.

" This is a very beautiful part," said Louisa, looking round. " There is nothing like this in the woods at Eltham. There are more shrubs there, and the trees are not so high nor stately; yet with all this beauty, Miss Isabelle, I feel very wretched."

" I shall be glad when we reach a house. It seems as though we were quite out of the world."

" I can see the end of the trees, I think.

Look. We shall be out of the forest soon."

In a few moments they emerged into an open glade. They looked around. It was like a meadow entirely surrounded by trees. The glade was probably about a mile long, by half a mile broad.

"There is smoke, and oh, thank God, there is a house," said Isabelle.

"So there is. Let us go to it at once."

They hurried forward, and after a little while reached the spot.

The cottage was built of mud, and thatched with reeds. The door stood open, showing the extreme thickness of the mud walls. As they approached, an old woman, hearing their voices, appeared at the door. Her face was wrinkled, her eyes dim, and her body bent with age.

"What do you want?" she asked.

"Let us rest awhile, good dame," said Louisa.

"Good dame! Aye, it is seldom I am called good dame by any one. There are very few hearts that are kind to poor old Eldie. Come in, come in."

Accepting the old woman's rough welcome, they entered. The cottage consisted of one room only, the smoke-dried rafters of the roof forming the ceiling. The room was sparsely furnished. A rough deal table stood in the centre. Two or three stools stood around. Beside the fire-place a kind of bench, constructed something like an arm-chair, was fixed to the wall.

"Sit in that seat, by the fire, my child," she said to Isabelle, who appeared to the old dame the more delicate of her two visitors.

"No, thank you, mother, this will do," said Isabelle. "I would rather see you there, for I am sure it is your accustomed seat."

"Well, so it is, my child. Bring the

8—2

stools closer to the fire, and sit and warm yourselves. And how is it you are such a way in the forest, and alone? Do you know your way back again? Where do you come from?"

"We have lost our way."

"The saints protect us!" said the old woman. "Well, you are welcome. My granddaughter has gone to the village for some things."

"What is the name of the village? Are we far from Eltham?"

"The name of the village near here is Chigwell. It is a very little place. I very seldom go there. The people hate me. They call me a witch."

"Have you lived here all your life?"

"I wish to heaven I had. I have lived in peace since I have been here; at least, such peace as I can have, remembering what I have seen in earlier years. I passed many years in France."

"Are we far from Eltham?"

"Yes. That is the other side of the river. We are about six miles from the river. Then you would have to cross it, and on the opposite side you would find Eltham. I know Eltham. The Earl of Draconbury lives close by there."

"Do you know the Earl of Draconbury?"

"Aye, I do. I can see now clearly before my old eyes things that happened years and years ago; not in this country, though. The Earl of Draconbury knows of them too. He was a bonnie master. I love his memory. There ought to be more like him. After the death of his wife his brother was killed, and he came home here, and has lived at Draconbury Hall ever since. I live on the money he gave me then, and I bless his good kind heart every day."

"Why do you not go and see him sometimes?"

"Because the sight of my face would

make his heart sad. It would recall his misery."

"I always thought he had some secret sorrow," said Louisa. "I have lived in the earl's service nearly two years."

The old woman started and looked fiercely at Louisa.

"Why did you not say that before?" she exclaimed, sharply; "I might have said more of the earl than he would have liked any one to know. But never mind, I have said nothing, after all."

"Do you know young Sir Ralph? He is the earl's nephew."

"No. I know the earl who was killed, and the present earl, and the Lady Rebecca—a pious fanatic. Here comes Elsie. This is my granddaughter. She was ten years old yesterday," said the old woman, as a child entered the hut.

The little girl looked shyly at the strangers, and walked up to her grand-

mother's knee, where she stood coyly examining the features and dress of the two
visitors. The contrast between the two
faces—that of the old woman and that of
the child—placed, as they were, in juxta-
position, was remarkable. No one, looking
at the bright hazel eyes, clear wax-like
skin, and finely cut features of the child,
would ever have imagined the little girl to
be a descendant of the withered and hag-
gard-looking creature who claimed to be
her grandmother. In a little time Louisa
and Isabelle, by means of their pleasing
manner and kind words, overcame the
shyness of the little maiden, and from being
distrusted as undesirable intruders, the
little creature ultimately looked upon them
as pleasant visitors and firm friends.

The old woman invited her guests to
partake of her homely meal, which they
did, relishing it greatly after their long fast
and exciting walk.

"Our best plan, Miss Isabelle," said Louisa, "will be to write to young Sir Ralph. If Sir Ralph knows where we are he will soon be here. How can we send a letter to Draconbury Hall?" she asked the old woman.

"A waggon passes through Chigwell every other day from Brentwood. You might send it by that to London."

Louisa took some silver from her pocket.

"If I give you this will it be sufficient to induce you to allow us to remain with you a day or two?"

"Bless the child! You are kind! But how can you sleep? I have only that little bed there for us all."

"If you do not mind," said Louisa, "we shall be satisfied with any accommodation, so long as you will allow us to remain until we can hear from Draconbury Hall."

CHAPTER X.

"*Alonzo.* What answer? Let me look upon that face
And read it there."
                                    THE REVENGE.

THEY had remained at the old woman's cottage two days. On the second morning there was a tap at the door, and before any one could rise to open it, Ralph himself walked in. Looking eagerly round the little hut, his eyes rested upon Isabelle. "My pet, my darling Isabelle," he exclaimed, as he kissed her passionately, "how kind to let me know where you were. Tell me all—how you came here, and why you left Hamil House. I went there the next night, as I told you I should, and Lady Claire was in a sad way about you."

" Did she so well dissemble that to you her sorrow appeared genuine ?"

" Her sorrow genuine, Isabelle ! What do you mean, darling ?"

" Did not the earl send for us to go at once to Draconbury Hall ?"

" The earl never sent for nor wished you to return."

" That was what her ladyship led us to believe."

A dark frown settled on Ralph's brow.

" I believe," said Louisa, " Lady Claire has played falsely with us. Do you know anything, Sir Ralph, of this necklace ?"

Ralph looked at the necklace. He saw at once it was one of great value.

" I know nothing whatever of it," he answered, " I never saw it before."

" This was given to Miss Isabelle by

Lady Claire, who said it was sent for her."

" By whom ?"

" She did not say. We imagined it came from you."

" There is some strange mystery in this," said Ralph. " Tell me exactly what Lady Claire said when you left."

" When we left ! You mean when she started us off. We were sent off at daybreak the morning before yesterday in her own coach. A man who spoke broken English drove the coach. We thought he was going to take us to Draconbury Hall, instead of which he came to this forest, and having induced us to alight, as he was going to rest his horses, while we were strolling a little way in the woods, he drove off with the coach."

" Well ?" said Ralph, for Louisa stopped.

" As we were looking about for the coach, that horrid dwarf appeared," said

Isabelle, "and said that Lady Claire had sent us here purposely to be rid of us, and also with a view of giving me up to his power."

"This is all most extraordinary," said Ralph, the frown on his face growing still darker. "Well, what followed, my dear Isabelle?"

"The wretched creature, with insolent speech, said that he was going to bind Louisa to a tree and take me away with him, but as he approached Louisa she stabbed him with a dagger."

Ralph looked at Louisa, the frown disappeared from his brow. He gazed at her with admiration.

"Was he killed?" he asked.

"We left him bleeding in the wood," said Louisa, faintly, for she dreaded thinking of the scene her memory recalled.

"I have heard of this dwarf before," said Ralph. "Is it not the same you fancied you saw beside your bed?"

"It was no fancy," said Isabelle, "it was he himself."

"It was the same horrid creature," said Louisa.

"Who is he?" asked Ralph, looking towards Isabelle.

"He was my father's servant. A man in whom my father placed the most implicit faith; but since we left London the hideous creature has been persecuting me, and seems as if by magic to know where I am, and appears when he is least thought of."

"Is he dead, do you think?"

"He may be," said Louisa with a shudder.

"At all events he does not know your retreat?"

"No. Even if he has recovered," said Isabelle, "he cannot know that we are here."

During this time the old woman listened

eagerly to all that was said, and never took her eyes off Ralph. The little girl sat in the corner, her bright blue eyes noting every action of the strange visitor.

"I must see. I must see," said Ralph, as though speaking to himself. Gently taking Isabelle's hand, he exclaimed: "Come with me a little way into the wood, will you, Isabelle?"

She arose, and they both left the hut.

As they strolled beneath the tall trees, Ralph exclaimed :

"Isabelle, I have thought over everything. I have looked at the step I am about to take from every point of view, and I am determined in the course I am about to pursue. I cannot be happy without you. Will you be happy with me, even if I never have more than sufficient to keep us as humbly as this old woman dwells here ?"

" shall be happy anywhere with you ;

but oh, pray consider what you are doing. Think of what you are sacrificing," said Isabelle, demurely, and with eyes cast down. "I should be happy, but you—"

"I have thought of everything, Isabelle. My aunt Rebecca is a religious fanatic, and notwithstanding her intense and gloomy piety, possesses a most inconsistent adoration for the empty forms and social distinctions of this world. But I need not describe her character to you. You have seen her. My uncle, the earl, is more reasonable—much more reasonable than Lady Rebecca, yet he has curious ideas of the value of birth. Anyone who has boldness to think for himself must see the absurdity of those petty distinctions — the advantage and superiority of high birth as it is called, is a phantom, but it has numberless brainless devotees. You love me, Isabelle. I know you do, and will be happy with me anywhere."

"I shall, Ralph, I shall," she said passionately.

"Bless your sweet tongue. It is the first time you have called me by my name."

"But think—oh, do not be too hasty—but consider long and well what you will sacrifice."

"I have thought of it, Isabelle, and have determined. I must ask you to remain here with this old woman and Louisa for a few days. I will inform the earl and Lady Rebecca of my intention. If they accede to my wishes all will be well, and I shall lead you back to Draconbury in happy triumph. If they refuse, (which I am afraid is almost certain,) then with the money I possess, we will cross over to France, and in your love, dear Isabelle, I shall find that happiness which will more than repay any disagreement with Draconbury Hall."

CHAPTER XI.

"Pulcheria. Who is that, that with such rudeness beats at the door?"

THE EMPEROR OF THE EAST.

ISABELLE and Louisa were the same night seated before the fire. The old woman sat cozily in her fixed bench or chair by the chimney corner, and the little girl sat on a stool at the feet of the two visitors, listening with childish delight to a fairy tale related by Isabelle.

Suddenly there was a noise outside as of some stealthy footstep.

"What is that?" cried Isabelle.

"Some one coming," exclaimed Louisa, looking around. "Surely Sir Ralph has never returned. Something must have happened."

The old woman looked uneasily at the door.

" No one ever comes here at night," she said.

Louisa arose and went to the little window. The shutter had not been closed. She looked out into the dark night, but could see nothing because of the light within. Shading her eyes with her hand, and peering more intently through the glass, she gradually made out a pair of eyes, which at first she took as the reflection of her own, but observing that they remained stationary while she moved her head, she watched them more narrowly, and finally, to her horror, traced the ugly features of Zermat.

" The dwarf! The dwarf!" shrieked Louisa, hastening from the window.

Isabelle went to the window, but could

distinguish nothing at all. The old woman too looked out into the dark night, but could see nothing. Notwithstanding Louisa's asseverations to the contrary, it was believed that she had been deceived. It was thought that her imagination, haunted by what had occurred in the wood, had deceived her vision.

The humble supper, consisting of bread, cheese, and onions, was eaten in silence. After this they retired to rest. The old woman insisted upon her two visitors occupying the only bed in the hut; she and her little grandchild sleeping on a mattress made of sacks and straw laid upon the floor.

When Isabelle and Louisa had retired to bed, lying so closely together they began talking in whispers without being heard by the old woman and child.

" Isabelle," said Louisa, " I am sure it was the dwarf's face. I am certain of it."

" If he knew where we were," said Isabelle, " I am afraid he would be making an attempt to carry us away. It cannot be Zermat. How should he know we are here ?"

Long after the regular breathing of the old woman and the child denoted their deep sleep, the two girls were engaged in conversation. As they were about falling off to sleep themselves, Isabelle exclaimed—

" What is that noise ?   Hark !"

" A footstep."

" Some one is sneaking about outside. It can scarcely be Ralph, or he would come in at once."

" God forbid that the dwarf has discovered us."

Louisa raised herself, leaning on one arm, to listen. There were unmistakable sounds of footsteps. She softly turned down the clothes, and got out of bed.

" What are you doing ?" asked Isabelle, in a whisper.

"Going to put something over the fire."

She took up a heavy sack, which served the purpose of hearth-rug, and placing it before the glowing, half-dying embers, shut out the little light they threw into the room.

"No one can see, now, through the window, what we are doing. Get up, Miss Isabelle, and dress yourself, but don't make any noise. If there is any danger, let us be ready. Thank Heaven I have this dagger still. I am sorry, now, I did not do more effectually that which a little while ago I was sorry I had done at all. I wish I had killed him outright."

"The dwarf! Oh, Louisa, do you think so? It makes me shudder when I think of his cruelty. Do you think it was his face you saw at the window?"

"I am certain of it. Do not speak too loud. Be quiet and dress quick. Hark! There is the step again. Listen!"

"I can hear a voice," whispered Isabelle. She had approached closer to Louisa, and clung to her arm as though for protection.

"There are more than one. There seem to be several footsteps."

"Oh that Ralph were here! God have mercy on us."

"Ralph should never have left us."

"But who would have thought we should have been discovered in this lonely hut? I am sure he acted for the best," said Isabelle.

"He ought to have sent Stephen or some one else to protect us. We are defenceless. The first one who approaches us shall feel this dagger—but what is one dagger in the hands of a woman against two or three men?"

They listened. There was no further sound of footsteps or voices.

"Perhaps they do not mean to come in,

after all. It may be no one who wishes to molest us," said Isabelle, hopefully. "Perhaps some wayfarers lost their way."

"Hush! not so loud. I hear them still."

At that moment there was a sharp rap at the outside of the door. Isabelle clung tighter to Louisa, and the latter put her arm around her companion, as though wishing to protect her from harm.

"What is that noise?" asked the old woman, in a sharp tone, suddenly awakening.

Louisa approached the spot where the old woman lay. Putting her head close to where she supposed her face would be, she exclaimed, "Some one is outside."

"Great Heaven! Who are you? Oh, I remember. Some one outside, you say. Stay; let me get a light."

"No, no. Don't do that. They will see us through the window. It is that dwarf come after Isabelle—the wretch we have told you about."

There was then a sharper and more impatient knock at the door, and a gruff voice exclaimed, " Come, Mother Barston, we want you. Come, open this door, you old witch."

" It has come at last," said the old woman, in a low, mysterious voice. " My time has come at last. Often and often have they accused me of witchcraft, and now the wretches want me."

" No, no—they don't want you, they want Isabelle and me. I am sure of it. It is that horrid dwarf, whose face I saw at the window during the evening."

" It may be—it may be," whispered the old lady, in a despairing tone, " but something tells me it is otherwise. My dream —that horrid dream—haunts me. But never mind ; let them knock. It will take them sometime to break through that door."

While thus speaking, she had dressed. She then put a heavy board before the window, and struck a light.

"They will see us through the chinks," said Louisa.

"There are no chinks nor cracks," said the old woman. "I took care to cover them all up long ago. Can I trust you two?"

"With anything," said Louisa and Isabelle, in a breath.

"You see that child sleeping there—my grand-child. Will you take care of her if I let you escape these wretches?"

"Willingly; but how can we escape?"

"Very easily. They will take me to the gaol. They have done so before, but I was released. After that I worked day by day——"

A thundering knock at the door interrupted the old woman.

"Do you wish me to come out to you in

my night-dress ?" she shouted. "Wait till
I am dressed, and I will come to you.
Eldie Barston is not one to run away. I
worked day by day," she resumed, "at a
pit beneath this floor. It will hold you
two and my child. See here."

She pulled the little bed on one side and
lifted two boards. There was a deep cavity.
A ladder reached from the floor to the
bottom of the pit, or cellar.

"This I meant for my own retreat. No
one ever dreams it is here. Take this light
and go down, and take with you my child."

"And you ?" asked Louisa.

"Never mind me. They will take me
away. When they are clean gone off
come up again, and you with the child
go at once away from the spot. Take care
of my child, will you ? You swear to
do so ?"

"I do. We do. But is it just to leave
you up here alone ?"

"Go at once. Here, take the light. Think no more of me."

The old woman then aroused the child, and taking her to the hole in the floor, Louisa carried her down the ladder. Isabelle followed. The old woman replaced the boards, and pushed the bed back into its place.

There was another impatient thumping at the door.

"Wait a wee bit, a wee bit. You shall soon come in."

She then unbolted the door. Zermat was the first to enter. In his hand he held a lantern. A malignant grin was on his face. He looked hastily round the hut, but when he saw no one there but the old woman a shade of disappointment and rage fell across his features. Two men followed him.

"We heard voices outside. Who were you speaking to?" asked Zermat.

"It is little odds to me what you heard."

"She was speaking to the devil, no doubt," said one of the men.

"I think I am speaking to him now," she answered, looking at the dwarf. "I believe I see before me one of his imps, or some old hell-dam's cub."

"Where are those two girls who were here this evening?"

"What two girls?"

"Those I saw through the window."

"You must not take any notice of what you saw through the window," said one of the men. "The old witch has power to raise up any shape or form in this room. Strange sights have been seen here by travellers."

"Aye—go on. My time may be come," said the old woman, "but neither you nor all the world can alter what is to be—cannot put forward my death one day, or put it back one day."

"She talks like a witch," said one of the men.

Zermat was looking round the hut. He was little disposed to believe in the old woman's power of raising up the beings he had seen through the window. He was certain he had seen Isabelle and her companion. While the two men were engaged taunting the old woman with her familiarity with the devil, he was examining the hut. In the course of his doing so he pulled aside the bed, and treading on the boards, noticed some of them were loose. He pulled up one. The old woman uttered a cry of alarm, and attempted to rush towards him, but was stopped by the other two men. Her cry was echoed by a scream from below.

"What did I tell you?" said Zermat, in triumph. "I knew I saw others through the window. They are down here. Bring the lantern. Bind the old woman in her chair."

The old dame was forced into the settle beside the fire-place, and there secured with a rope. They then took the lantern, and, preceded by Zermat, descended the ladder, where they found Isabelle, and Louisa, and the child, huddled up in one corner clinging to each other, and trembling with fear.

CHAPTER XII.

" *Werner.* Retire: I'll sift this fool."

WERNER.

" YOU say you went to the cottage and found it forsaken," said Stephen, sitting on a truss of hay in the stables at Draconbury Hall.

"Yes," said Ralph, whose pale face and features denoted the intense mental anguish he had suffered. "I could find no trace of them at all. The most mysterious part of it is that pit beneath the hut I told you of."

"I cannot understand that pit myself."

"There was everything as I had seen the room before, with the exception of the bed pulled from its place by the wall, and beneath it those boards up, and a ladder leading down into the pit."

"Did you make enquiries in the neighbourhood ?"

"Neighbourhood !   There is no neighbourhood only what is covered with forest trees.   It's all forest.   At the nearest village I found that the old woman was considered to be a witch, but even that information goes for little, for the stupid people could scarcely understand which hut I meant."

"It is almost a pity you came back."

"You mean, I should have continued my search for them."

"Yes.   Every moment gives him further time to get away."

"I came expressly for you to accompany me.   You must go at once, Stephen.   We must find them."

"But what will the earl say at my absence ?"

" Never mind that. I will take all blame."

" Have you told him that they were sent away from Hamil House ?"

" I have told him nothing, Steeve, neither do I mean to tell him anything. If he knew about it and my aunt too, there would be no end of deliberations, and it would be night before we set out. I am satisfied if we start at once we shall be upon their track before night."

" Very well, Master Ralph. I will risk the earl's displeasure, or anything, for you."

In a little while the two rode out of the courtyard of Draconbury Hall. Little notice was taken of their departure, for it was their custom to ride out once or twice a day for a gallop in the forest.

When clear out of the view of the house they urged their horses forward at their utmost speed, keeping their heads to the north for the bank of the river.

"How shall we get across?" asked Stephen.

"It will be awkward," said Ralph, "but the first barge we see must take us to the other side."

In a little while they could plainly see the sails of a craft upon the stream. A sailing barge was tacking close in to the Kent shore. The men on the barge answered their shout. The shore was fortunately steep, so that the vessel was run in close to the bank without grounding. It was a work of time and difficulty to get the two animals on board. The bargemen, aroused by the sight of a guinea, tasked all their ingenuity to accomplish this object. At last, making a kind of platform or gangway from the bank to the barge with planks which they had on board, the two horses were got safely on deck. When this was done the wind, which was keen and brisk, soon wafted them across the river to the Essex shore. The bargemen ran their boat high up the shelving bank of mud, for they said they could well afford to wait for the flood tide to float them off again. In disembarking, Ralph's horse floundered completely in the mud and water, but received no injury. In a little while they were both remounted, and hastily galloping across the flat marshes in the direction of Chigwell.

When they reached the village Ralph again made enquiries, but could learn nothing of the fugitives.

"Let us go on to the next place," said Stephen. "It will be the best thing to do. We must make a rapid circuit round the forest."

"That would take some time. I think he would be certain to go north or east, because those directions are right away from London and from Draconbury."

"Would he try the river?"

10—2

"I should think not. Let us go off to the next place—Ongar."

They rode on some distance.

"There's a fellow trimming this road ditch," said Stephen. "He would notice pretty well every one who has passed along here this morning—that is, if they have passed since daybreak."

When they reached the spot where the man was at work, Ralph exclaimed: "Have you noticed two ladies pass along the road, friend—one about twenty with dark hair, and the other younger with golden hair?"

"Golden hair," said the fellow, putting his hand to his back and gradually raising himself into an upright position. "Well, no," he said after a pause, as though attempting to remember. "Golden hair. No. It's a sort of hair as ain't very common. The only girl as I have heard on lately with golden hair, is the one as was collared with old Eldie Barston, just out here in the forest."

"What!" shouted Ralph, with such energy that the man started, exclaiming : "Lord save us, what is the matter?"

"Where is she? Quick! Tell me."

"Well, they are all at Ongar, and—"

"Come on," said Ralph, and followed by Stephen he galloped furiously along the road, while the ditcher looked after them in amazement. In a little while they came within sight of the village.

"Here is a decent-looking house, shall we stop here?" said Stephen, pulling up at a little tavern about half a mile from the village.

"It will be the best plan," said Ralph, "to make further enquiries."

Dismounting and giving their steeds into the care of the ostler, they entered the tavern and walked into the public room. No one was there save one stranger, who was sitting on a bench with his knees curled up so as almost to touch his chin; he was apparently fast asleep. Ralph looked at him, and from the description given of Zermat by Isabelle, he felt convinced that the being before him was the dwarf himself. He stepped back quickly, and motioned to Stephen not to enter.

" There is the villain himself—the dwarf —curled up in the corner asleep. Peep," whispered Ralph.

Stephen cautiously looked round the door, and returning declared it was the very same fellow who had fired at the earl in the forest—the same fellow he had captured, but who wrenched himself from his grasp and escaped.

" You get what you want in the kitchen, Steeve. He may recognize you again. He has never seen me. He will not know who I am. I will sound him as to where Isabelle is. This is a most providential meeting."

Ralph then entered the parlour, while Stephen repaired to the kitchen.

"What orders, sir?" asked the waiter.

"Any cold meat you may have, and a tankard of the best ale," said Ralph, at the same time purposely knocking over a chair, so as to arouse the dwarf. Zermat started up, and, rubbing his eyes, looked wildly around.

"I beg your pardon, sir," said Ralph, in his most fascinating and courteous tone; "I am afraid I have abruptly terminated your slumber."

"Sir," replied Zermat quickly rising to his feet, and bowing low, for he was highly flattered by Ralph's apology; "Sir, I perceive you are a gentleman by your urbanity, and I am proud and happy to meet you. Pray do not apologize for the noise. I certainly was asleep, but your arrival is most opportune, for I am sure I have slept quite long enough."

"I should be extremely sorry," said Ralph, "to inconvenience any gentleman."

"I am certain you would, sir. The good humour of your face proclaims the geniality of your soul."

"I am proud to receive such a compliment, sir," exclaimed Ralph, thinking how he should like to clutch the fawning reptile by the throat. "Have you travelled far ?"

"I was travelling all night, sir."

"Will you consider it impertinent if I ask you to join me in my homely meal ?"

Zermat, on the contrary, considered it very kind. Although he had many gold pieces in his pocket, his parsimonious nature led him eagerly to accept the invitation.

The waiter brought in the refreshment, and Ralph and the dwarf, after a few more formal and unmeaning complimentary speeches, sat down together. Ralph did not fail to well replenish the dwarf's glass every time it appeared to be getting low.

After the meal he suggested wine. Zermat was equally willing to indulge in that luxury at the expense of the stranger.

"I dare say," said Ralph, "you may be surprised at my asking you to join me, but the fact is, I have been absent in France for some years, and having just returned to England, I am only too glad to obtain the society of my fellow countrymen. What village is this just beyond here?"

"Ongar, sir. It is the spot where all my hopes are centred," said the dwarf, warming with the wine.

"How so?"

"Because there is confined in a common gaol—in a miserable barn—a detestable hovel, the most beautiful girl you ever saw —imprisoned, sir, and imprisoned upon one of the most unfounded of charges—the charge of witchcraft."

Ralph looked keenly at the dwarf's face. It was flushed with wine. He believed that even if he did betray a little anxiety, it would be unnoticed by his deformed and vinous companion.

"But who is this girl who has so disturbed you, my friend?" asked Ralph.

"One that I love greater than my life."

"But if she is confined in so miserable a prison, surely you might rescue her—if it is a mere barn or hovel, as you say."

"What am I, single-handed, against all the village? They tried to burn them in the barn, last night."

"Them! Then she is not alone there."

"No, there are others with her."

"Why are the villagers so revengeful against this girl?"

"Listen. This girl, and her friend, and an old woman, and a child, are all accused of witchcraft. The fools of clodpoles believe they are all connected with Satan, and wish to put them to death at once."

"It must be a great trouble to you. Take some more wine."

"It is, very," sighed the dwarf.

"Is the object of your love very beautiful?"

"Beautiful! She is an angel. Golden hair and bright blue eyes, cheeks like a pale young rose, and lips like cherries. Her name is Isabelle. She is as graceful in her movements as a young fawn."

Ralph started.

"What is the matter?" asked the dwarf, gazing vacantly round with his heavy wine-laden eyes.

"Nothing. I nearly upset my glass, but fortunately I have saved it."

"She is indeed a beautiful creature," said the dwarf, dreamily; "and the worst of it is this—that it is all through my own folly she is locked up there."

"That is inexplicable."

"It may seem so, but I can easily explain

it. I love the girl. Her parents detested me. They sent her away with a friend into the forest, thinking I should not be able to find her. At least not her parents, but people who had charge of her. The whole of the story is too long to tell you. But I discovered them. They had taken refuge with this old woman, Eldie Barston, or some such name as that. I was afraid to attack them single-hand, for one of the wenches, not Isabelle, stabbed me with a dagger, so I got some men from the village here to help me, and the confounded headborough gave an order that they should all go to prison, and, in spite of all my entreaties, poor little Isabelle is there with them. But I have a plan of rescue. Sir, by your dress and manner, I assume you are not unacquainted with the science of war."

"I have seen no rough, actual service, although I have been in one or two slight brushes, but I am nevertheless pretty well acquainted with the sword. I should like to join you in this rescue, if agreeable to yourself."

"You have just divined the request I was about to make. I thank you greatly for your offer."

"When is it to take place?"

"This very night. There is no time for delay. I must have a horse ready. I must go and arrange for that now," said the dwarf, rising. "I will meet you at dusk, and then we will survey the place where they are confined. At midnight we will make the attempt. Sir, accept my most humble thanks for your services. Adieu till we meet again."

"Adieu."

The dwarf, making a low bow, strutted out of the room. Ralph looked through the window, and watched him out of sight. He then went into the kitchen, where he found Stephen sitting by the fire.

"Do you, think, Master Ralph, he would know me in this disguise?"

"I scarcely knew you myself," said Ralph. "He has gone out for a little while, but he has communicated everything. Isabelle is at Ongar, locked up with the others. He is going to rescue her, and has solicited my aid. At dusk we are going to reconnoitre the place where they are imprisoned. You follow us. Your disguise is good. It almost deceived me. You follow, and you will see where the place is. Then at midnight we are to make the rescue. At midnight you bring the two horses, and be close at hand."

"Don't you think, Master Ralph, it would be better to go to the headborough at once, and tell him all?"

"That would consume too much time. Furthermore, would he believe me? How could I convince him that my tale is true? True, my uncle is the Earl of Draconbury,

—that might have some weight—but would he believe us unless we fetched the earl himself? That would take too much time. No, no, I prefer assisting this wretch. When once I get sight of Isabelle, a pistol shot will settle the villain."

Stephen shook his head doubtfully, but said nothing.

CHAPTER XIII.

" Don Pedro (aside). Heaven grant me power to
stifle my rage till 'tis time to let my vengeance fly !"

THE FALSE FRIEND.

A T dusk the dwarf returned to the inn.
"I have settled everything," he said ;
" shall we go at once and have a look at
the barn ?"

" Is it a barn they are confined in then ?"
enquired Ralph.

" Yes, and therefore the more easily
broken into."

They then started off and walked towards the village. Ralph now and then
caught the sound of Stephen's footsteps following.

"I think there is some one behind us," said the dwarf, stopping to listen.

"It can be of little consequence if there is. If our design were suspected, they would be at the barn to protect it."

"True, I never thought of that. Your brain, my dear sir, is quick and clear."

They walked on in silence some time, when suddenly the dwarf exclaimed: "That's the barn," pointing to a rough wooden building standing in a field about one furlong from the village.

"My plan of action is this," said the dwarf. "There is one man on sentry at the door in front of the building. You or I must go there to him, and demand admittance, and manage somehow to throw him, and gag, and bind him. Then, with no one to disturb us, a few of the rotten old boards will be quickly moved—it will be very little trouble. Can you devise a better plan?"

" Why not take the keys from the man,
and open the door ?"

"Because he does not carry them. He
is simply a sentry, that is all."

" In that case I do not think your plan
can be improved."

" I am unable to express my gratification
for your promise of assistance."

" Do not speak of it. It is one of those
cases in which I feel most deeply interested."

" Thank you—a thousand thanks."

They turned again and walked towards
the inn. Ralph was debating in his mind
whether it would not be better to act upon
the suggestion of Stephen. This so occupied his thoughts that he failed to observe
his silence was noticed by his companion.

" You seem dull, sir," said the dwarf.

" Indeed," said Ralph, "I must apologise.
I was thinking of something that happened
abroad many years ago. But here we are
at our quarters. I will ask you to join me

in another bottle of wine, and then you must excuse me till the time you appoint for the rescue. In the interim I must write some letters."

"With all my heart," said the dwarf, gaily.

Ralph, when the bottle was finished, left Zermat in the parlour and adjourned to the kitchen, where he consulted Stephen as to the course he should pursue. Deliberately and carefully they viewed the matter from every conceivable point of view.

"I think after all, Master Ralph," said Stephen, when they had thoroughly exhausted the subject, "it will be as well to act as you have proposed yourself."

"We can do no otherwise now. To denounce the rascal to the authorities would take time, and in a couple of hours or so he will probably have Isabelle in his power. Surely, Steeve, we can out-wit and overpower this miserable epitome of humanity.

11—2

Our success will rest much upon you, Steeve. Bring both our horses out about ten minutes after we have left, and take up your position near the barn where you can see, or at all events, hear, what goes forward."

"Trust to me, Master Ralph. There are two things to be done. Miss Isabelle must be rescued, and this dwarf must be slain. You attend to the former, and leave the latter to me."

Just before midnight, the dwarf and Ralph left the inn. The old innkeeper's curiosity was considerably aroused, but a guinea quickly subdued it, or at all events prevented any importunate question from crossing his lips.

"It's very dark," said the dwarf, as they walked cautiously along.

"It is the better for our enterprise. Where is your horse ?"

. "It will be there."

They walked on in silence the rest of the way.

"I can see the barn now," said the dwarf. "We will wait here a little while for the others."

"Others! What others?" asked Ralph, fearing he was outwitted already.

"Why, you see, my friend," said the dwarf, "in the last two hours I have not been idle. My brain works quickly. The girl herself is not very partial to me, and probably would resist going away with me. Now I have done this: I have been in the village, and obtained a contingent—in fact, a little army. Thirty or forty of the villagers are coming, thinking to burn them all as witches. First, with their aid, we shall overpower the guard, and even if the constables of the village come, we shall be more than a match for them. In fact, we shall be masters of the position. Well, Isabelle's terror of them will make her

cling to me. Once get her on my horse
and I will trample them all down. Hark !"

Ralph heard the dull irregular beat of
several footsteps, and a distant hum of
voices. At first he was dismayed by Zermat's intelligence, but a few seconds' reflection led him to believe that the dwarf's
altered plan would be all in his favour.
The tramp of the villagers became more
distinct, and soon a dark moving mass approached, at first indistinguishable, but
ultimately resolving itself into the outline
of several men armed with clubs, sticks,
scythe blades fastened on poles, reaping
hooks, hatchets, and other strange and
quickly improvised weapons. These ugly-
looking things, and the savage yells and dis-
cordant cries and shouts of the half mad
rabble, made Ralph shudder as he thought
of Isabelle and her position. He vainly
regretted he had not taken Stephen's advice
at first, and at once handed Zermat over to

the headborough. The crowd, when they saw the dwarf, set up a howl of delight and recognition.

" Lead us on, master," said several of them. " 'Uds life, we'll have a bonny fire to-night, and the devil shall have his own again."

While Zermat was speaking to the excited mob, Ralph slipped away from his side, and unseen by anyone by reason of the darkness of the night, went to the clump of trees where he had previously arranged Stephen should stand with the horses.

" What is all that noise, Master Ralph ?" asked Stephen, in dismay.

" Heaven preserve us, Steeve, we are outwitted. That scoundrel has obtained the aid of this mad mob to assist him in rescuing Isabelle from the barn, and then, on the plea of carrying her to a convenient spot to be burned, he means to get her on his horse and ride away with her."

"We must ride after him. There will be two to one."

"I know. But imagine these infuriated demons having her in their power."

"We must assist the dwarf in his strata- gem, Master Ralph, and then follow him."

"That is our only course, but these infatuated brutes may in their frenzy at once proceed to maim her and the others with their terrible weapons. They are all armed with scythes, reaping hooks, and sticks, and clubs."

"We must prevent that. We must keep near to Isabelle. Between us we have eight pistol shots. I doubt if any of the wretches have a gun amongst them."

"I think not. They seem to have seized every farm implement that first came to hand. You must come with me. Leave the horses here and follow me, but do not join the crowd till their attention is thoroughly engrossed. Remember—endeavour by all means to assist the dwarf in taking Isabelle clear of the crowd. Then we will run here, mount, and follow him. I do not think his hack or his horsemanship will equal ours. Hark! There is another shout! The bloodhounds! Quick —follow—cautiously."

Ralph soon rejoined the throng, and reached Zermat's side.

" Where have you been? I missed you all at once," said the dwarf.

"I thought I saw a light just beyond there, and went to see. What are you going to do? I suppose these fellows are completely under your control. They will not murder them at once when they see them?"

" No. I have been addressing them. They will do as I wish. I have moulded their rough will to my wishes wonderfully. Instead of burning them I have suggested that each one—the old woman, the little

child, and the two girls, which includes
Isabelle—God bless her—"

Ralph nervously clutched his dagger.

"I have suggested," continued the dwarf,
"that they should all be tried by the
ancient ordeal of walking over hot plough-
shares. This delighted them very much.
Burning would only last a certain time,
but this kind of torture could be prolonged
to any length, and the fools gloated over
their anticipated night's amusement.
Halloa! here's the sentry gagged and
bound."

Three strong fellows brought up the
miserable watchman, who had been pacing
in front of the barn. His hands were tied
behind him, and in his mouth was stuffed
his own handkerchief, a piece of rope passing over the front of it and being tied
behind his head.

"Here he is—here he is, master."

"Lay him down on one side," said Zermat, "do not harm him. Some one will find him in the morning, and release him no doubt. Lay him down under that hedge there. Now, my lads, you with the hatchets, come forward and break through these boards. Stop. Before you begin one word. No one enters the barn but me. This gentleman here will stay with you. I will enter and bring out the prisoners. It will be better to proceed with something like military precision."

"Right, sir. Right," said a dozen voices. "Now then, here's to the devil's dam."

"Have you altered your plans?" asked Ralph in a whisper, half mad with rage at being obliged to dissemble and truckle to the miserable wretch beside him.

"A thought has just struck me," said the dwarf, "I will go in alone. These fools will all be waiting here. It will be easy with a hatchet to force the lock of the door, and I can take Isabelle and walk out unobserved, and ride away with her."

" But they will hear you force the door," said Ralph, who scrutinized every project with extreme caution, not because of any regard for the dwarf, but by reason of his anxiety for Isabelle's welfare.

" I will avoid that, you will see."

During this time half a dozen axes had been thundering at the boards ; the crashing and splintering noise of the yielding wood was accompanied by screams of alarm and terror from within. In a very short time there was sufficient room for a man to enter.

" Now, my lads, stop—that will do !" shouted the dwarf.

Ralph was surprised at the influence he possessed over the crowd.

" Now, my men," resumed the dwarf, " I will go in. I am not afraid of witches nor of their great master, the Devil. While I am in sing the doxology. It will counteract any incantation these witches may perform against any of you."

Then arose a steady, monotonous chant —the ignorant hinds actually believing that they were assisting in a combat between the powers of light and darkness.

"That will drown any noise I may make in forcing the lock," said Zermat to Ralph, "you see my brain works quickly. I will go in, and leave by the door. Sir, I am obliged to you for your kind assistance. I will rest with my horse a mile on the road beyond the inn where I first met you. I should like to see you again. Good bye." Then, calling out aloud, he exclaimed: "Give me an axe."

One of the men stepped forward and held out the desired weapon, all the while vigorously and piously chanting the doxology with the others. Zermat then entered the barn.

"Isabelle! Isabelle!" he cried.   He received no answer.   He stood still and covered his eyes with his hand for a minute. After this he could see much more plainly about the place.   He reasoned they would be in the furthest corner from that part of the barn which had been broken through. He thought he could discern in the farther corner a patch of white.   He approached it.

"Isabelle! Isabelle!" he whispered, "I have come to save you."

"The Devil take such saving as yours," cried a voice which he knew to be the old woman's.

He moved closer to the spot whence the voice sounded.

"I wish to save you all," he said.   "You hear that crowd.   They are the villagers going to burn you all.   I have pretended to be of their opinion and with them in their design, but I have a plan for your escape."

" If you were the cause of our capture why should you suddenly wish for our escape?" said a voice, the tone of which made him shrink back instantly, for it was the voice of Louisa, and he remembered the dagger. His shoulder was still smarting from the wound.

" Isabelle !" he said, " I have discovered your father. Come with me and see him."

He listened for a reply, but none came. He would have gone nearer but for that dreaded dagger.

" Isabelle !" he resumed, " do you prefer death—do you prefer being burned and butchered by these mad savages, to going with me and seeing your father again ?"

He listened, but there was no answer.

" Isabelle ! do you hear those brazen throats chanting that dirge ? That will prove your funeral dirge if you stay. They are all for this moment religious fanatics. They believe you are witches, and that to burn you will be a religious duty. Think of those heartless ignorant brutes standing round piling up the logs and feeding the flames as they lick your face, and scorch your skin, and turn those pretty blue eyes into cinders., Think of all that. Can you not sooner trust me than that crowd of savages ?"

There was a pause of some moments.

"Go with him, child," said the old woman. "Go with him. What he says is true. Those fellows outside mean mischief. They will think no more of burning your dear body, than they would of roasting an apple."

"Oh, my father! my father!" sobbed Isabelle, "where is he ?"

"I will take you to him," said the dwarf, at the same time attempting to impress upon his hearers the certainty of his promise being fulfilled by such a terrible oath, that both Isabelle and Louisa stopped their

ears, and the old woman murmured:
"Mercy on us!"

"Will you trust me?" he asked.

"Louisa must come too, then," said
Isabelle.

"She may come, of course. Come, be
quick. They are getting impatient. I can
take you out at the door and slip away
unseen. Where are you? Give me your
hand."

A hand grasped his outstretched arm.
He pulled the owner towards him, and was
about to kiss her face, but his head was
thrust roughly away by a strong hand, and
the voice of Louisa exclaimed—

"Keep your ugly lips to yourself, or you
will remember it."

Zermat raised the hatchet to strike her,
but he let it fall again harmless to his side.
He reasoned it would be better first to get
Isabelle out of the vicinity of the mob;
afterwards he would deal with Louisa. He

flattered himself that he was more quick-witted than she was.

"Isabelle, take my hand. I swear to protect you."

"She has hold of my hand," said Louisa. "Lead the way."

Zermat led them from the corner. He thought it would be best to get out of the barn at once. The vigour with which the doxology had been chaunted was gradually abating. It was evident they were getting tired of waiting. He reached the door, and inserted the edge of the axe between the lock and the door-post. It quickly yielded, and the door swung open.

"Come along," he said. "Be quick, or they will see us." Taking Isabelle by the hand they ran for shelter behind a hedge, closely followed by Louisa. As the latter was swiftly running, the dwarf dexterously thrust out his foot sideways, which caused her to fall. In a second he had stooped down, and wrenching the dagger out of her hand, hurled it a hundred yards from the spot.

"Now you can do what you like," he said.

He seized Isabelle again by the hand, dragging her along at a swift rate.

"Louisa—where's Louisa?" she cried.

"Hush, you little simpleton! Do you want those wretches to discover and burn you?"

In another moment he lifted her on to a horse, and springing up into the saddle himself, trotted the horse forward into a lane thickly overshaded with elm-trees.

Louisa got up half stunned by her fall, and looked about for the dagger, for she had not seen the dwarf hurl it away. Then she hastily followed Zermat and Isabelle, and reached them just in time to see the horse trot away with its double burden.

In the meantime Ralph had not been inactive. The moment Zermat entered the barn Stephen had been within ear-shot disguised as he was, and having heard much that was said, hastened to the side of his young master. Ralph quickly explained what Zermat was about doing, adding—

"I shall follow the villain alone. You stay here, and try to save the lives of the old woman, and the child, and Louisa. Reason with these fellows. Point out the dwarf's treachery. They will see they have been duped. At all events, I must go at once."

He ran to the clump of trees where the horses were tied, and to his dismay could find no trace of them.

"Duped again—fooled—outwitted! God help that dear girl!"

He was just about rushing back, when the neigh of his own horse, which had heard his voice, led him to the spot.

Unhitching the rein from the branch of a tree, he jumped into the saddle, and rode ϯ to the spot mentioned by Zermat.

CHAPTER XIV.

"Not so long and wide the world is,
Not so rude and rough the way is,
That my wrath shall not attain him,
That my vengeance shall not reach him!"
THE SONG OF HIAWATHA.

RALPH, as soon as he gained the high road, urged his horse into a fast gallop. He passed the inn where he had first met the dwarf. In another three minutes he was in sight of the place of rendezvous, but neither horse, nor Zermat, nor Isabelle could be seen. All was quiet and silent as the grave, save the wind sighing through the trees.

A fiery heat suddenly rushed through

his veins, as he thought that the dwarf
might have duped him.

"Fool! fool!" he cried, "he may have
gone another road.   Why did I not enter
the barn with him, and running my dagger
into his false heart, find Isabelle and bring
her away?   Oh, my God! I have been in-
sane these last six hours!   My wits must
have left me to act as I have done!"

In another moment he reflected that
having started several minutes before the
dwarf could have possibly found Isabelle,
forced the barn door, and found and
mounted his own horse, there was nothing,
after all, so very remarkable in finding himself first at the place of meeting.

Presently he heard the canter of a horse.
The sound grew louder and more distinct
every moment.   He strained his eyes in
the direction of the village, and before long
he could see an object approaching.   He
was the moment afterwards able to discern

the flutter of Isabelle's white dress. He pulled out his pistol, and wheeling his horse into the middle of the road, he awaited the approach of the dwarf.

"Here we are, my kind sir," said Zermat; "I am much obliged to you for your——"

"I shall be much obliged to you, sir," said Ralph, "if you will release that lady, and——".

"Oh, Ralph! Ralph! is it you? Thank God! thank God!" cried Isabelle, immediately she heard Ralph's voice.

"Isabelle, my darling, I am here to protect you. I have tracked this——"

A pistol report rang through the night air, and Ralph fell from his horse.

Isabelle uttered a loud shriek of terror, and fainted.

Zermat clutched her fragile form closer towards him, and digging his spurs into the horse, urged him forward at full gallop.

He gave a low chuckling grunt of delight as he murmured—

"If people used more powder and less words they might fare better. I suppose he was going to summon me to surrender, as a general would a fortress he was about to besiege. It is a wonder he did not stop to write down an order summoning me to deliver up this proud little minx. By my holy star, is it possible that I have been all this evening in the company of this same Ralph? I have heard of him, but what a meek-hearted chick he must be; a score of times he might have trounced me—spitted me like a frog, but he didn't. Well, he has lost his life, and lost his sweetheart, and earned his death, by thinking that words are equal to powder. Come, Isabelle—come, darling, cheer up. A sigh, ah, that's better. You will open those dear blue eyes soon to see me before you. Why the devil doesn't the girl love me? If she won't, I'll break her proud young spirit yet."

Ralph lay in the road apparently dead. His horse stood quietly beside him, sniffing and blowing with its dewy nostrils over the pallid upturned face of its young master. Twice it neighed as though calling for a response from those pale cold lips which had so often spoken to it words of fondness and endearment. Presently it raised its head and pricked its ears, and then gave a loud neigh. Again it looked down at its master, and then started off at a quick trot in the direction of the village. The cause of its movements was soon apparent. Coming along the road was its own stable companion, bearing Stephen with Louisa, whom he had rescued, sitting before him. The noble brute, with curious instinct, trotted up to its approaching companion, and then turning round, appeared about to join it in its progress towards the spot where Ralph lay.

"Great God!" said Stephen, "what, young Sir Ralph's horse! He is killed."

"Oh, don't say so," said Louisa, in alarm. "Heaven grant that he is not."

Stephen urged his horse into a sharp gallop. The other horse kept by his side, neighing and snorting as though the noble creature wished to communicate the sad intelligence of his master's condition.

The man soon arrived at the spot where Ralph lay. He dismounted, and raising his master's head, found him still breathing. Presently he opened his eyes, and said faintly, "Stephen."

"Yes, Master Ralph, it is me. For Heaven's sake what is the matter? Your head is bleeding."

"Shot," said Ralph, "that dwarf. Raise me up. I am coming round."

Louisa got some water from the little rivulet which trickled along by the side of the road, and in a few minutes he was

sufficiently recovered to stand on his
feet.

"I am stunned," he said. "That villain.
He has gone with Isabelle."

"We must follow him. Can you mount
your horse?"

"Yes, yes. I am much better. It is
snowing. Thank God we shall be able to
track his horse's footmarks. That poor
girl! she cannot come with us."

"Oh, Sir Ralph, do not trouble about
me," said Louisa. "I can walk to, the
next house, and obtain shelter."

By a tremendous effort Ralph partially
shook off the effect of the fall.

"Give me a lift into the saddle, Stephen,"
he said. "Now take Louisa before you,
and let us go on to the next house, where
we can leave her."

The snow fell thick and fast as they
pushed forward. Ralph's wound was a
slight one, the ball just grazing his skull,

and peeling off the skin, but it had been of sufficient force to stun him. He grew rapidly better. Presently they reached a house on the roadside, where, after a little delay, they left Louisa; giving the old woman who opened the door a guinea for her trouble.

"Now, Stephen, we must push along faster. I feel myself again. Thank Heaven for this snow. There is his horse's track, you see."

".We shall soon come up with him, Sir Ralph. No doubt he thinks you are dead, and he never dreams there is any one else to follow him, for he did not recognise me through my disguise."

"Where did you find Louisa?"

"Just by the trees; and the old woman and the little girl escaped somewhere. I saw them going by a hedge, while the fools were burning the barn, thinking they were inside."

"Thank God they are safe. Come along, come along," said Ralph, impatiently. "Watch well his track that we do not miss it."

They then pushed forward rapidly. Presently they came to two diverging roads, where they alighted to examine the track.

"Here it goes, to the left," said Stephen.

They remounted, and plunged down the narrow lane, maintaining a rapid gallop, until the hoof-marks they were following turned suddenly on one side, and were lost in a broad, shallow ditch.

"He anticipates pursuit evidently," said Ralph, "see, the crafty hound, he has crossed the ditch."

"He never plunged through the hedge, there," said Stephen.

"It looks as though he had. See how the snow is disturbed, and the bushes bent backwards. In my opinion he has gone across the country."

"No, Master Ralph, no horse ever went through that hedge, or over it, in the last two hours. No doubt he thought himself very clever when he beat about the snow and bent down the twigs and briars, but it would take a more crafty fellow than he is to deceive an old woodsman like me. No. He has walked his horse either onward or backward along the ditch. You look one way, and I will look the other. Watch for the least sign."

Ralph retraced his way along the edge of the ditch, while Stephen proceeded in a contrary direction. In a few minutes the latter cried, "Here it is; here it is."

Ralph hastened to the spot, and found the water of the ditch running through a wide bed of short rushes; part of them stood upright, furred and glistening with the white virgin snow. There was a patch, however, of about two feet square, where no snow appeared to have settled, and in one part the rushes seemed to have been crushed down. Stephen stood down in the ditch, his heavy boots partly in the water, his hands on his knees, and his head bowed down, intently looking at the rushes.

"No horse can have passed there," said Ralph. "I half believe, now, he must have got through the hedge yonder."

"You are mistaken, Master Ralph, he has leaped his horse over this bed of rushes, but the animal has not quite cleared it. This patch here, where the snow is knocked off, is where his hind feet have struck."

He stepped farther into the shallow water, and baring one arm, examined with his hand the bed of the stream.

"Yes, Master Ralph, here is where he has been. I can feel the two holes in the sand and pebbles where his feet have struck. I am as sure of that as I am of my own existence."

Stephen quickly regained the bank, and

mounted his horse. They then walked up beside the ditch, watching for any evidence of the dwarf's horse having left the water. For some time they followed the stream, until at last it ran into a large open waste of water by the road side, extending some considerable distance back towards the verge of the forest.

"What now?" asked Ralph, looking anxiously at Stephen.

"This is awkward," said the keeper. "Stay. What is that mark there?"

In an instant he was down from his horse, and examining a narrow black patch in the roadway.

"A footprint, Master Ralph, and a lady's, too. Here is another and another. Here it goes. By Heaven it comes straight from the dyke."

Ralph dismounted, and looked with beating heart at the delicate, tiny footmarks. "These prints must have been made by

Isabelle," he said, his heart palpitating wildly.

"I see it all, now," said Stephen. "He has made her dismount, and walk round this water, to a distant point, while he forded it on horseback. He thought by that means to hide the horse's track. Now, Master Ralph, we must follow these foot-marks."

"The accursed wretch!" said Ralph, passionately, "to make one so tender wade through the cruel cold snow."

"But how could he persuade her to assist him in this scheme?"

"He has held the vengeance of the villagers, and the burning stake, as a terror over her head."

"We must follow these steps. Here they go. Thank heaven for the snow. In less than twelve hours we shall have dealt out justice to the scoundrel. After this, Master Ralph, no doubt we shall find he went on straight, thinking he had done sufficient to baffle any pursuers."

The foot-prints led them a long dreary way round the sheet of water. Ralph shuddered when he thought of Isabelle wading at that time of night' through the snow. Presently they found the footsteps suddenly turned to the water's edge. There were also the marks of horse-shoes, and of heavy big boots.

"You see," said Stephen, "he has dismounted to assist her to mount. Now, here go his horse's feet, and I'll warrant they will go pretty straight now."

As he predicted, the track of the horse kept to the high road. They now made up for lost time, and galloped rapidly forward. The road still ran direct south, and after a long ride they knew by the marshy character of the land, they were approaching the river.

"If he has crossed the river it will be

awkward," said Stephen. "Look, here comes a horse. It is his no doubt."

"Whose horse is that, my good fellow?" asked Ralph of the man who was leading the animal by the rein.

"It can make little difference to you," was the gruff answer.

"Come, come," said Ralph, good-humouredly, "it is not difficult to answer a civil question."

"The question wasn't civil at all. It was impertinent, and deserved the answer it got."

"It is not your horse?" said Ralph sharply.

"I have the charge of it nevertheless."

"Who gave you the charge of it?"

"One whose purse is well lined with gold, and who pays well for what is done for him."

"You mean a miserable and deformed wretch."

"How do you know that?"

"With a young girl. Have they crossed the river?"

"If you want him you will have to cross after him."

"Come, come, Ben," said Stephen, speaking for the first time, "fetch out your boat and put us across the river. We shall pay you quite as liberally as the hunchback."

"Who calls me Ben?" asked the man, quickly moving closer to Stephen, and attempting to get a better view of his features in the darkness.

"Why Stephen Barfleur, and this is the nephew of the Earl of Draconbury. Be quick and—"

"The Earl of Draconbury! No money will I take from any one belonging to him. May his life be long and happy. He bought me my first skiff when I was as poor as a tramp."

"A young lady was with the rascal you have just taken over?"

"Yes, a sweet pretty girl, Stephen. I did not take them over. I sent my son with them. The hunchback wished me to stay on this side, and prevent any one crossing, for at least two or three hours. He told me a tale of being pursued, but now I find one belonging to the house of Draconbury pursuing him, I know who is in the wrong. The Draconburys have never yet been guilty of oppression. They are too ready to fight on the side of truth, whether it is to benefit prince or beggar. So here goes the dwarf's gold," he said, flinging first one guinea and then the other into the marsh dyke beside the road.

"Don't throw the money away, man."

"Gold from such a fellow as that, and for such a job as that, is like a witch's blessing—it does one more harm than good."

"Let us get across at once," said Ralph, impatiently. "We can talk when we are in the boat.   My brain is on fire with this delay."

" Never fear, sir.   My son is strong, but I can still overhaul him.   They have but just started, and we shall be on the Kent shore pretty well as soon as they."

" You've got another boat handy ?"

" Yes, but it's up high and dry on the mud.   It'll take the three of us to launch her."

" Then, for heaven's sake," said Ralph, " let us do it at once.   Here Steeve, fasten the three horses to this stump.   Take care of our horses, old fellow.   You will hear from us again.   The dwarf's you can keep. You will never be troubled with him any more.   Now then, we are losing time."

" We shall be at the other shore as soon as they."

" We don't want that," said Stephen.

" Why not ?" asked Ralph, impatiently.

' It will be better to let them get out of

sight, into the woods. We can follow their track. If the dwarf sees us in pursuit he will be using his pistols at us while we cannot fire at him for fear of hitting Miss Isabelle. Besides, in his haste, finding he was outdone, he might shoot her."

" The accursed wretch !" growled Ralph ; "but I believe you are right, Steeve."

" We must land a little above or below them. When we find their footsteps it will be easy to trace their track and take him by surprise."

They had now reached the top of the river wall, and the broad waters of the Thames were before them.

" Do you see that little speck there ?" said the boatman, "right away there? You can't ? Well, your eyes ain't so used to speering about in the dark as mine. Here's our craft. Now then. Heave-hoy !"

The boat slid along the mud on her keel at every heave of the three men, and soon her stem clove the water, and the moment afterwards she floated buoyantly on the surface of the stream, saucily throwing up her head for the opposite shore, until a tug at the painter, which the old man held, brought her inshore again.   He held her stem while Ralph and Stephen jumped in, and then leaped in himself.   He took hold of the oars, and the first stroke he gave showed that he had not over-rated his power.   The little skiff shot forward at each pull of his brawny arms, with a bound, the bows ploughing up the water, the sharp whistling sound of the spray showing how fast they were going.

"Lie down in the boat," said Ben.   "It is always lighter on the water than it is on the land.   Lie down close or else perhaps if they see another boat with three in it, and if he expects any one after him, he may think it's you."

Ralph and Stephen lay down at the bottom, while the man rowed away lustily.

"You may get up now," he said, after a little while. "We are close inshore. They can't see us against the bank. Now, gentlemen, step sure—mind—be careful—this way —jump—that's right. Now walk along there till you come to where they have landed. You will see the snow trampled down. They have been ashore above two minutes. I can see Jack is just putting back for the other side. The young rascal hasn't seen me. I'll rate him for this. The dog has been asleep; but perhaps they kept him occupied with talking too much."

"I can't see any boat, Ben," said Stephen.

"I don't suppose you can, friend. If you had passed well nigh forty years on the water as I have, you would have a keen sight and a keen ear for anything on its surface, or beneath it either. I dare say now, you would beat me at seeing a rabbit or a pheasant. Everyone to their trade, friend."

"Take these three guineas, friend, and

stay here for an hour or so.   We may want you," said Ralph.

"What for ?" asked Stephen.

"I have thought of a plan. We can talk of it going along. Let us be off at once."

CHAPTER XV.

"Epilogue. Besides, if thief from gallows you reprieve,
He'll cut your throat."
LOVE IN A WOOD.

THEY left the old man sitting in the boat, clinking the guineas one against the other, and listening to the pleasing ring of the metal—a sound that brought up before him visions of many a bonny piece of beef and tankard of foaming ale.

They hurried along the bank of the river watching eagerly for the least sign of disturbance in the pure white snow. After a little while they came upon footmarks.

"Here is where they landed!" said Stephen, "and here go the footmarks right across the marsh here towards the woods."

"Let us follow them. Keep a sharp look out, and not a word, for we cannot be far behind them."

They followed the footsteps. · It was easy to trace the long, slouching gait of Zermat and his big feet, beside the delicate footprints and shorter steps of Isabelle.

"She has a pretty little foot," said Stephen.

"Come on, for heaven's sake. Quicker —quicker. See here they go to the wood. Who knows how the wretch may be this moment illtreating her. Oh, heaven, cool my brain ! I shall go mad."

"Be calm, sir."

They followed the footsteps some distance into the wood, as they wound in and about the bushes and between the trees.

"Hark ! what is that ?" whispered Ralph, stopping short and detaining Stephen by the arm.

They both listened. The loud tones of a

harsh, stern voice sounded through the wood.

"He is threatening her," said Ralph. "Creep behind me, Stephen. I will put a bullet through the villain's head."

"Be steady, Master Ralph; mind you don't hit her."

"Never fear, Stephen. Now I have reached him—now I am so near my nerves are of iron—now I know he is in my power."

They cautiously approached the spot whence the voices sounded.

"There they are," said Stephen, "come behind this bush. Look, there they are! Good God, he is holding a pistol at her, and she is kneeling down on the cold snow."

"Oh, father! father!" sobbed Isabelle, "oh Ralph!—will no one help me?"

"Call on that name again and I will fire," said the dwarf, in a voice tremulous with rage and hate. "Ralph, as you call

him, is dead. You know I shot him.
Swear by all the saints in heaven—swear
—promise that you will be my wife.
Promise. I will give you two minutes to
consider."

"I cannot fire," whispered Ralph, "my
bullet would go too close to her. The
least movement of her head would bring it
within the range."

"Come farther this way. Stop. Not a
whisper, mind, or he will hear us."

They stooped down and crept behind
some low bushes. Twenty paces brought
them into a position from which the ugly
figure of the dwarf was seen in profile
standing in front of Isabelle.

"Remember! two minutes you have to
consider," said the dwarf, dropping his pistol
to his side and taking one step backward.

"Now!" whispered Stephen, who held
his own pistol ready in case Ralph's shot
was ineffectual.

A sharp report echoed through the woods. A fierce howl of pain and rage arose in the stillness of the night.

" He is down !" said Stephen.

In a second both Ralph and the keeper were on the spot. As they approached, Zermat raised his arm and fired. The ball went through Stephen's hat.

" Villain !" he said, pointing his pistol at the dwarf. " Die ! You loathsome reptile —die !"

"Stay," said Ralph, " don't shoot him. Let him live. I have not done with him yet. Take his pistol from him."

" Oh mercy ! mercy ! my shoulder is crushed !" cried the dwarf, writhing in pain.

" Mercy forsooth !" said Stephen, " you imp of Satan. Ask the Devil for mercy ; you have need. Your life will soon be ended."

As he was speaking he stooped over the dwarf and wrenched the pistol from his hand, and a dagger from his waistband, though not without great resistance on the part of the prostrate dwarf.

"What is this rope round your waist?" asked Stephen.

"Oh my back!" roared the dwarf, "water! water!"

"I don't object to your keeping this rope, friend," said Stephen, "but I will put it round you in a different way."

He bound him hand and foot tightly and securely, and left him groaning with pain.

In the mean time Ralph had been attending to Isabelle. On hearing the pistol shot, she had fallen on the snow in a swoon. Ralph rested her head upon his knee. Her eyes were closed, and her long golden hair fell in rich clusters upon the snow. He passionately kissed her pale lips, calling out her name, and using every means in his power to restore her. Gradually she recovered. She opened her eyes, but although they gazed up into Ralph's face, she did not seem to recognize him.

"Isabelle! Isabelle! it is Ralph who is with you. Do you know me. Come, Isabelle, my darling—my love!"

"Thank heaven!" she murmured. "Oh, Ralph—take me—away—from him. Don't leave me."

"Nothing but death shall part us after this, Isabelle. Are you better?"

"Much better. Oh, Ralph, is this a dream—is it true?"

"It is no dream, Isabelle," he said as he kissed her rapturously.

She clasped her arms round his neck and clung to him with passionate fondness.

"You never will leave me again, Ralph?"

"Never—never—by heaven."

By this time Stephen joined them.

"Has she recovered, Master Ralph?"

"Yes; thank heaven. Do you know who this is, Isabelle?"

"Yes; he was at the Hall."

"Yes, miss. You remember me?" said Stephen. "You are safe now. Let's get her under shelter, Master Ralph, as soon as possible. This is a sharp night for any one to be out in. See, yonder is Shooter's Hill up there. Here is a light away here through the trees. Perhaps we might get shelter for her there. Give her to me, Master Ralph, I can carry her; don't you tire yourself. Lor! bless you," said the honest fellow, as he lifted Isabelle up and sat her on his arms, as though she had been a little child, "a man as can carry a sack of corn for a mile or more, ain't likely to be tired with such a lovely burden as this. Put your arm round my neck, miss, and lean your head on my shoulder. It will rest you."

They soon reached the cottage, and knocked at the door. It was some time before it was opened; for the inmates, after

they had been aroused, devoted some minutes in reconnoitring from behind the
blinds and through the keyhole, the appearance and nature of their untimely
visitors.

At last the door was opened by an old
man, who inquired in a trembling voice
what they wanted.

"Can you find shelter for this lady till
daybreak?" said Ralph. "She is almost
exhausted with exposure. I will pay you
whatever you wish."

"You will find it to your benefit, old
man," said Stephen. "No one ever yet
complained of the illiberality of the Earl of
Draconbury."

"The earl! Come in, come in. Bless
you, 'tis the earl who gave me this cottage."

They both walked into the little room,
and Stephen placed Isabelle in a chair with
great tenderness, and with a degree of so-

14—2

licitude for her comfort that contrasted strangely with his brawny frame and rough exterior.

"Poor thing," said the cottager, "she is pale and cold. I will go call my old lady, and we will soon have a fire and something hot for her. Take a seat, gentlemen, both of you, and make yourselves at home, as if ye were up at the great Hall. No, ye cannot do that, for the place is humble, and the victuals too, but what there is use it as your own."

"We cannot sit down," said Ralph; "we must go for a little while. We may be absent about an hour."

"Are you going to leave me here?" asked Isabelle, in some alarm.

"I shall return in about an hour. You are safe here, Isabelle, darling. That hideous dwarf is bound hand and foot. He will never trouble you again."

Isabelle shuddered.

"You will be as safe here, miss," said the cottager, "as if you were up at the great Hall—quite as safe. You heard that dog barking when you were knocking? If I were to set him on to any one, he would be a dead man in a few minutes. Besides, no one ever comes here, miss."

"You are not afraid to stay, Isabelle?" asked Ralph, taking her hand affectionately.

"My nerves seem crushed. You will not be long, Ralph?"

The peril of the last few hours and the exciting events had thoroughly removed her maiden shyness.

"No, pet. Good-bye for a little while," he said, kissing her.

He then left the cottage, followed by Stephen. When they had got a few paces he stopped and exclaimed—

"I am half afraid to leave her now. But nothing can happen to harm her. Do you think she is safe?"

"She will be safe, Master Ralph. Let us go and despatch this wretch. Why did you not wish to have him shot?"

"You will see."

As they approached closer to the spot where the dwarf lay, they heard his terrible groans and calls for help, mingled with blasphemous imprecations.

"The wretch can see death before him, and shudders at the sight," said Ralph.

When they reached the spot where he lay, and he saw them approaching, he implored them in piteous tones to spare him.

"I will give you gold—all the gold I have, if you will let me live," he exclaimed.

"Gold is of no value to me," said Ralph, "I have more than I wish for now. Why have you persecuted Isabelle?"

"Because I love her."

"Monstrous presumption!"

"But you love her yourself."

"I have never persecuted her. You were

with her father.   You are her father's servant."

"Her father is Merlin.   Spare my life,
and I will tell you the secret of her birth."

"You know no secret."

"Promise me my life."

"Who are her parents ?   Not Merlin ?"

"No.   She was born in France."

"You do not know more of her history,
I see, than I do.   You have no secret to tell."

"I can tell you something of Lady Claire."

"Lady Claire is nothing to me now."

"She sent Isabelle away purposely from
Hamil House."

"I know she did."

"I have many secrets that would be
valuable to you.   You shall know all if you
will let me live."

"No, your time has come.   The devil
will not be cheated of his due any longer.
How far away are we from the river,
Stephen ?"

"Not more than three or four hundred paces, I should think, by the winding track we made from the boat."

"Don't drown me," shrieked the dwarf, "I hate the water. Oh, God! don't drown me!"

"Take the wretch by the shoulders, Stephen; I will take his feet. I scarcely like, though, to touch such carrion. We will carry him to the river."

"Mercy! mercy!" shrieked the dwarf. "I will tell you all—everything."

"Stop such howling, or I will strike you with my pistol," said Stephen.

They picked him up and carried him towards the river.

"Oh, God, have mercy on me!"

"God has nothing to do with a demon like you. Address your prayers to Satan. You will soon meet him."

"Oh, spare me! I will do anything! Mercy! mercy!"

"You shot the earl," said Ralph; "you shot at me—you shot at Stephen there— you have been a curse to Isabelle ever since Merlin was shut up in the Tower. How can you expect mercy?"

The dwarf gave a deep groan of despair.

They reached the bank of the river, and found the old boatman sitting in his boat a few yards off.

"Bring your boat ashore, old fellow," shouted Ralph.

"What have you got there, master?" asked the man, as he brought the boat to the spot where they were standing.

"A mass of iniquity that will soon be at the bottom of the river," said Ralph. "It is almost a pity that such a grand and majestic stream should be polluted by such a reptile."

"Oh, Lord, spare me!" groaned the dwarf.

Taking little heed of Zermat's frantic appeals for mercy, which were strangely intermingled with curses and imprecations, he was, by Ralph's orders, placed in the boat. He was still bound hand and foot, and lay, as they placed him, helpless at the bottom of the little skiff.

"I may as well tell you," said Ralph, "what we are going to do with you. You are going to be sent adrift with the tide in this boat. We have pulled out the cleaning cork, so that the water will slowly trickle in, and in about half an hour you and the boat will sink quietly to the bottom of the river—the proper place for such heartless villains as you."

"Oh, spare me! Pray! Shoot me—anything—I hate the water."

"You will have half an hour or an hour for reflection, and to overcome your hate."

"I will pay you for the boat," said Ralph, to the boatman. "Shove her off well into the tide so that he may sink in deep water. It is an act of divine justice to rid the earth of such a loathsome thing."

The boat was shoved off well from the shore, and, being taken by the tide, drifted into the middle of the stream, and down towards the sea. Its outline soon merged into a shadowy mass, and became more indistinct every moment to the eyes of the three men who stood watching the living bier from the shore ; but the yells, oaths, and maniacal ravings of the doomed man within it were heard long after the fatal skiff was lost in the gloom of the night. They stood some time listening to the terrible shrieks of the dwarf. Suddenly they ceased.

" He has become resigned to his fate," said Stephen.

" He has gone under," said the boatman. " This gentleman told him he would be half an hour going down, but I knew the boat would fill through that hole long before that time. He is down at the bottom now, and, however bad his deeds, he has paid a fearful penalty."

"You are right. It is a terrible penalty —but his badness deserved such a dread retribution," said Ralph. "Take this money, friend, and if you will kindly keep our horses for a day or two, I will send or come for them, and pay you for your trouble."

"I am well paid, sir, already; but I should not care for such a job any more. It will be sometime before I get those death-shrieks out of my ears."

"How will you get across?"

"My son is on this side, sir; I signalled for him to come over. I shall go back with him."

"All right. Good night, friend. And now, Stephen, let us hasten back to the cottage."

CHAPTER XVI.

"*Gulnare.*   This is the missing link !
With this the web of mystery we'll unravel."
                                   THE MASQUE OF STAMBOUL.

A SHARP walk soon brought them in
sight of the cottage. The smoke
was curling up from the chimney, and a
bright light was gleaming through the window.

"It looks cheerful within," said Ralph.

They knocked at the door, and were admitted by the old woman. They found
Isabelle sitting before a roaring fire. On
the table stood some mulled ale and toast.
The cottager's wife, a happy-looking old
dame, with bright eyes and silver hair, was

busy performing many little duties to en-
hance the comfort of her young guest. Isabelle looked round at Ralph with a sweet
smile of welcome ; but the next instant her
features assumed an expression of anxiety
and sorrow.

"I am so glad you have returned," she
said.

"But you look sad. What is the matter, darling?" asked Ralph, taking a seat
beside her.

"I have made a discovery since you left.
You see this," she asked, holding up a
quaint home-made cap. "This belonged
to my old nurse, Margaret, of whom you
have often heard me speak. She is upstairs asleep. She has been staying here
ever since my father left London, but it
seems father went out one day, shortly after
they came here, and has never been seen or
heard of since. It was thinking of him
that made me sad."

"This is extraordinary that we should happen to come to this cottage. Then you have not yet seen the old nurse—Margaret?"

"No; they wished to wake her, but I thought she had better not be disturbed till the morning."

"I will wake her at once," said the cottager's wife, "I am sure she will soon get up to see you. She has talked of nothing else, miss, since she has been here but you; and when her old master disappeared and never returned again, and she was left here alone,. I thought she would cry her eyes out."

The old woman then went upstairs, and was away some time. Ralph and Isabelle sat together talking of her father, while Stephen partook of the good things on the table, making a hearty meal after the night's work.

In a little while Isabelle heard footsteps

on the stairs. Her heart beat quick as the steps reached the door. She turned and saw old Margaret enter the room. The meeting between the good-hearted old woman and her nurse-child was warm and passionate — the old nurse laughing and weeping for joy, scarcely able, in her excessive delight, to answer the many and anxious questions put to her by Isabelle, respecting her father.

" Who is this ?" asked Margaret, after a little while, looking at Ralph.

" This is—" said Isabelle, but she blushed and said no more.

Margaret looked hard at Ralph. She stared so long that Ralph could scarcely help smiling at the old woman's rude curiosity. Not satisfied with the view she got of his features from the place where she sat, she arose, and, taking the light, examined his face with such intensity of interest that Ralph laughed outright.

"Well," said Margaret, putting down the candle, "if you had been ten or fifteen years older I should have sworn that I had seen you before."

"Where?" asked Ralph, highly amused.

"Miss Isabelle," said the old woman, "I know you have heard that Merlin is not your father, although he has acted the part of one ever since you can remember, and I know he loves you as fondly as ever any father could love his own child. You recollect what he told you about your mother."

"Yes," said Isabelle with deep interest.

"I nursed your mother. I did not nurse her from the first. The nurse who was there when you were born died, and I was engaged to fill her place. I was engaged because I was an Englishwoman, and was there with an English family. You were some months old when I first attended your mother. I only saw your father once. He only called once, for your poor mother died suddenly. He who called was the exact image of this gentleman."

Ralph now became deeply interested himself. A flush of joy shot through his heart. He had heard of his uncle's strange marriage in France. Was it possible that Isabelle could be his daughter?

"My uncle is about the age you describe," said Ralph; "and I happen to have with me now a miniature of his taken some ten or twelve years ago. See, here it is."

Old Margaret took the portrait eagerly, and stared at it intently for some moments, holding her breath the while. The expression of her features was one of extreme intensity. Her eyes were dilated, and her lips firmly compressed. At last she exclaimed—

"Miss Isabelle, my darling, my love, whoever this man is—whoever he may be— he is your father; he is the man who came to see your poor mother for the last time."

" Impossible !" said Ralph.

" I say again," cried Margaret, looking round steadfastly at the circle of faces, which were all viewing her with astonishment, for the old cottager and his wife, and Stephen himself, were listening with wonder to the extraordinary disclosures, " I say again, whoever that man is, he is the father of this child—of Isabelle."

" He is my uncle, the Earl of Draconbury," said Ralph.

" I did not know him by that name," said Margaret, " but that is the man, I will swear."

" Oh, Isabelle ! Isabelle !—Joy ! joy !" shouted Ralph, rising and kissing her with rapture, " my own sweet cousin ! At daybreak we will go to Draconbury Hall. Nothing can now prevent our marriage. Bless you, Isabelle !"

Isabelle was so bewildered she could say nothing ; but seeing so many faces looking

15—2

at her, she bowed her head in confusion, and kissing Ralph's hand, bedewed it with tears of joy.

"You must go with us to the earl's, madam," said Ralph. "He will be rejoiced to find his daughter again, especially in one so fair and beautiful, and one for whom he has shown much regard. Isabelle, my darling, when Lady Rebecca finds you are so nearly related to her, you will find her nature much altered. She will love you."

"I am afraid," said Isabelle, "her heart is too cold to love any one much."

"At all events," said Ralph, gaily, "there will be no objection now to our marriage. What a grand one we will have, Isabelle! The only thing now remaining to be accomplished is to find that good old man you love so well—Merlin."

"My father," said Isabelle, "at least I always thought he was my father. I hope God will assist us in finding him. How

strange if the earl really is my father. I
have always loved him,—he has been so kind
and good to me since he first found me in
the wood."

" But how is it," said Ralph, thought-
fully, and with a slight amount of gloom
and anxiety in his face, " how is it that the
earl did not recognise the portrait which
you had of your mother as being the portrait of his wife—the miniature you showed
him, Isabelle ?"

" The portrait Isabelle has got," said
Margaret, " is not the portrait of her
mother."

" You always said it was, Margaret," exclaimed Isabelle, in astonishment.

" Forgive the deceit, my dear girl ; I did
so. I thought the portrait of your mother
was too valuable for you to have. I believed it was the only link by which we
might one day discover your father. I
thought it was too precious to be trusted

in your keeping. You might have lost it. I have always kept that myself. It has always been fastened in my bosom. See, here it is, Isabelle, my love. I admit that I have deceived both you and your father— I mean Master Merlin—for he never actually saw your mother, but I know both you and he will forgive the cheat I practised. It was done for a wise and good purpose. See, here it is."

Ralph and Isabelle eagerly looked at the precious miniature which the old woman produced. It was the portrait of a woman in the flower of youth and beauty. The features bore a striking resemblance to those of Isabelle. There was the same bright rich golden hair, the same soft blue eyes, and the same sweet quiet repose about the lines of the mouth.

" Was that my mother ? Dear mother !"

ᵀsabelle, fondly kissing the trinket, as ed tear fell upon it. " And she died, Margaret?" she asked, in a choking voice.

"My darling Isabelle," said the old woman, solemnly. "God is mysterious in his ways. What we once thought a terrible tribulation, has now proved to have been a blessing. Had Merlin never gone to the Tower we should, perhaps, never have been so near discovering your father as we now are."

"But did she die?" asked Isabelle, anxiously.

"She died," said Margaret, sadly and solemnly.

Isabelle bowed her head, and for some time the little circle was hushed in silence.

"Come, my child," said the old cottager's wife, after a while, "dry those pretty eyes, and take some of this warm ale. Remember you have had no rest, and the following day will be another sad trial to your strength."

CHAPTER XVII.

"*Brutus.* I think it is the weakness of mine eyes,
That shapes this monstrous apparition.
It comes upon me.   Art thou anything?
Art thou some god, some angel, or some devil,
That mak'st my blood cold, and my hair to stare?
Speak to me, what art thou?"

JULIUS CÆSAR.

ON the night of the day that Ralph and Stephen left Draconbury in search of Isabelle, the earl and his sister Rebecca sat in the great hall taking their evening meal.

"Ralph is late," said Lady Rebecca in her usual stony tone. "Where can he be?"

The earl summoned one of the servants, and asked if Ralph had been seen lately.

"No one has seen him since three o'clock, my lord."

"Humph," said the earl.

When the servant had retired Lady Rebecca looked towards the earl and exclaimed : "Brother. I think Ralph's conduct of late has been somewhat strange. He is often absent many hours, and returns late at night."

The earl readjusted the wick of the massive lamp that stood on the table, as he exclaimed : "He is the same as all boys are, Rebecca. You cannot expect boys to stick indoors as girls would."

"No one wishes him to stick indoors," said her ladyship, "whatever that elegant phrase may mean, Thomas ; but I think he might say when he was going out, and where he was going, and when he would return."

"Just what a man never knows himself, Rebecca."

"You attempt to palliate everything he does, brother. You seem totally unconcerned as to his welfare."

"I think, Rebecca, Ralph is old enough and wise enough to take care of himself. The fellow has got the old Draconbury blood in him, Rebecca, and will never be a milksop. I am proud of him, Rebecca, and you ought to feel so too."

"I can never be proud of any one who thinks so lightly of the death of his fellow-creatures."

"I believe Ralph is as considerate of life, and as just and generous as ever holy writ wishes man to be."

"Have you forgotten his zeal in storming Sir Gilbert's house?"

"And have you forgotten Hampden, Cromwell, Fairfax, the Earl of Stamford, Nathaniel Fiennes, and others—have you forgotten their zeal and the thousands they slew?"

"You cannot compare Ralph to those holy men, Thomas."

"It is unnecessary to do so. Measure

one act by another. Surely you do not wish to argue that because a man is ostensibly pious that his acts are not to be questioned."

" But they delivered the nation."

" And Ralph released a captive from heartless oppression."

" A wandering girl!"

" Nevertheless a human being and a fellow-creature."

" This discussion will be useless, Thomas."

" It is a subject on which we never agree."

" Because you will grope in the dark, and never seek the light of truth. The dust of the world is in your eyes. You cannot discern the beams of holy light when they are thrown across your path."

" Not when the beams come from such a gloomy lantern as yourself, my sister."

Lady Rebecca arose, and walked with silent and solemn grandeur from the great hall. The earl smiled as he heard the heavy door close behind him, and then relapsed into a reverie.

About half an hour after Lady Rebecca had retired, he was startled by a noise at the door. He turned and beheld an object which sent a thrill of horror through every vein.

It was a female figure, clad in a coarse serge cloak, fitting tight to the throat and gathered in at the waist by a girdle. Her pale face bore the marks of long suffering, yet it was evident that when young, and before trouble and sorrow had so seamed it with lines of care, her features must, indeed, have been beautiful. Her large pale blue eyes glittered with peculiar lustre, rendered more remarkable by the absence of all vivacity and life from the other features of the face. Her hair, which fell unconfined by ribbon or plaits over her shoulders, was white as snow.

The earl started up and stood staring at

the apparition, speechless with amazement. There was something in the face he remembered, yet he could not tell where he had seen it before. It seemed a face well known to him—a face that had haunted him for years, as though in a dream. The slow, noiseless, gliding walk of the figure, would have led one less strongly nerved than he, to believe that the mysterious visitor came from another world.

" You may well be surprised, my earl of Draconbury," said the sad lady, in a low and sorrowful voice. " It is fifteen years since you last saw me. I have changed much, but I remember your features, for you have not changed as I have. It was at Paris I last saw you. Do you remember Charles Stuart and Annette ?"

"Annette ! Good God ! You are not Annette !" said the earl, starting back.

" I am that same Annette. I was decoyed away from there by a heartless

villain, who has just gone to meet his
Maker. I have been imprisoned—confined
in one room since then till a few hours ago.
Charles Stuart, as I have only just heard,
is king of England."

"Great heaven, madam, be seated! Is
it possible—it cannot be possible that you
are still alive!"

"I am still alive, my lord."

"But we were told you were dead—I
was told you were dead. Who decoyed
you away?"

"Sir Gilbert Dubois."

"What, the man who is just dead—the
man who lives close by here — here in
England! Impossible! This must be some
mistake — yet those features. You are,
indeed, Annette."

"I am, my lord."

"But what induced him to imprison
you?"

"I will tell you all that happened. I

received a letter purporting to be from you.
It requested me to meet you in the woods.
I was surprised at the request, but I thought
probably you disliked again entering the
house where your wife, poor Alice, had died.
I went to the place mentioned. There I
was seized by some ruffians, and brought to
England, and placed in Sir Gilbert's house
—in a room level with the lake. I have
been a prisoner ever since."

"But why was all this ? It seems—"

"Sir Gilbert afterwards with fiendish
malice told me why I was seized. He
believed I was your wife—he had discovered
how much you loved Alice. He mistook me
for Alice. He did not know she was dead.
You had incurred his fiendish enmity, and
he seized me to be revenged upon you."

"The dastard !"

"I told him I was not your wife, and
that Alice was, who was dead ; but he
laughed at this, and said it was an ingenious

ruse, but one that would fail to deceive him. I have been a prisoner in his house till now."

"But why did you not send to me, or to the king? Surely you could have done that."

"Why did I not make known my imprisonment, you ask. Because, my lord, I was kept a close prisoner in one room all those years, never seeing or hearing of any one but my jailer."

"But you have escaped at last."

"When the tyrant died his wife released me. I left her house this morning and I enquired for you at the neighbouring village; for Sir Gilbert, to increase my torture of mind, long ago told me that I was within a little distance of your dwelling. When I got to the village this morning, I thought I would start here at once. Afterwards I determined to defer my visit till daylight had gone."

"There was no necessity for that, madam

—Annette—I will call you Annette—I will send to the king at once, and let him know that you are still alive."

"Pardon me, my lord. The king is no longer Charles Stuart. He is now the king of this land, and he is lawfully married. Why should I disturb his quietude by again recalling to him his youthful follies?"

"But he loved you passionately, Annette."

"And now loves another. No, no, my lord, I do not wish to see him now. I only wish to remember him as he was then—as he was when he was my first love."

"Perhaps you may be right, Annette. Neither he nor I have much to be proud of when reflecting upon our stay at the French Court. Events which then happened have thrown a shade over my life. You know the king and I were boon companions then. We have quarrelled since. He accused me of carelessness in matters concerning you. You will remember what occurred. He was

imperious in spirit and hasty in language.
He used harsh terms. I too, I regret to
say, possessed all the fiery spirit of the
Draconburys, then uncurbed by the reason
which age and reflection bring to us all.
It was only my extreme loyalty to the house
of Stuart that prevented me from crossing
swords with Charles, who is now our
king."

"My only object in calling upon you, my
lord, is to enquire after my child."

"Alas, madam, it died."

She bowed her head, and with her hands
clasped on her knees, sat some moments in
silence.

"God rest its soul," she said, in tremulous
accents marked with deep emotion, and
showing how great had been the effort of
her will to control her feelings.

"My lord," she at length said in a firm
voice, yet tinged with melancholy sadness,
"my work on earth is done. The lady who

released me from my terrible imprisonment graciously gave me a purse of gold sufficient to carry me to France. She wished me to stay in her house, but I preferred going to the nearest village, as I have said. I shall now return to the village. To-morrow I set out for France, to find, I hope, with the mercy of my blessed Redeemer, that calm and leisure for prayer and repentance which will alone fit me for a future world. My lord, I give you my heartiest gratitude—"

"Be seated still, madam—Annette, be seated—you must stay here till the morning at least. My sister, who is a good pious creature, may comfort and console you. Stay and rest yourself, I pray—I beseech you, madam, do so. I am bewildered by this sudden appearance of one whom I have thought dead so long ago— of one who was the sister of—"

The earl stopped, for, strong man as he was, his emotion overcame him.

16—2

"Of your wife," said the lady, solemnly. "She is in heaven."

"Oh, Annette," said the earl passionately, "consider that to me you represent the only earthly link betwen that dear creature and myself. Do not leave me, pray. Stop, if only—"

He ceased speaking, and clasping his forehead with both hands, murmured in passionate grief: "Oh, God! oh, God! this is terrible."

Bowing his head he wept with that fearful convulsive emotion that only strong men exhibit when their nerves are broken down.

"Do not weep, my lord," said the lady, in a sweet voice of sympathy. "Calm yourself. My sister is a saint in heaven."

"She is—she is," said the earl fervently, raising his head and making a strenuous effort to control his feelings. "She is. Oh, Annette, I was just to her. We were lawfully married. I was poor then. My brother held the estates. He has since died. He died abroad while intriguing for the king's return. I did not announce to the world that I had married, for many reasons —foolish and stupid I think them now, but which I then considered, in my hot-brained youth, sufficient to induce me to keep our marriage secret. Poor Alice, her life was short. Annette! Annette! answer me before God, faithfully and truly. Did you ever think it was I who poisoned her?"

"I will answer you truly. Yes, I did; but only for a few moments. When I saw your passionate grief I knew you neither did it nor consented to such a cowardly act."

"God bless you for that, Annette."

"My lord, I afterwards discovered something further, but which I never told you at the time, for I believed you too impetuous to sift out a clue with sufficient coolness and skill. I intended to have done so myself, but was seized by that cruel tyrant.

Your wife, poor Alice, was poisoned by a woman."

"A woman !"

"A woman who loved Charles Stuart. She was jealous of me. I was the intended victim, but poor Alice took the draught. The woman mistook her for me. Alice and I were much alike, sufficiently so to induce a stranger to take one for the other."

"You were. Who was this fiend? Did you ever hear ?"

"I never heard her name. But I saw her face just as she was leaving my poor sister's room. Ah !" she exclaimed, looking across the great hall, but looking with a peculiar gaze that seemed to be fixed upon an object far beyond the wall of the room, "that face—I see it now—a face that seemed to beam with the soul's light. It was a sweet face to cover such a cold cruel heart. That face I shall know it, if ever on this side of the grave I meet it again. Enough, my lord. This recalling of the past is painful to us both. It is useless. I have no object to live for now, but to make my peace with God. I would rather this moment bid you adieu, my lord."

"Nay, nay, stay I entreat you."

"I implore you, my lord. It is useless my staying. It will only prolong your grief."

"Surely you will grant—"

At this moment the door opened, and Lady Rebecca entered. As soon as she observed a stranger, and so strangely dressed, she stood fixed to the spot. The earl arose in confusion; the strange lady arose also, and bowed reverently to Lady Rebecca.

"Rebecca," said the earl, in a sad, low voice, "I have told you before all that occurred at Paris. You remember all I told you of that place."

"I do. Is this your—"

"This is the sister of poor Alice. Her life has been one of sorrow and tribulation."

"Every one's life is [full of sorrow, brother," said the stony-hearted Puritan. "Some make their lives more full of trouble by the path they tread."

The stranger shrank from her gaze, and involuntarily moved so as to increase the distance between herself and the cold-hearted woman. The earl noticed her movement.

"Rebecca," he said, "if you are human, for heaven's sake show a little sympathy for one who has suffered so much."

"I will, my lord. Let me converse with the lady alone. Leave us together and I will give her spiritual consolation."

"Madam, I will retire," said the stranger, in such a firm and sonorous voice that Lady Rebecca was startled. "I will ask God for that kindness and mercy which he always gives when addressed in a humble and broken spirit. I wish to trouble no one on earth with my woes and sorrows. I appeal to God himself. I appeal to no earthly mediator."

Lady Rebecca was abashed. The earl bit his lips with rage—rage because of his sister's stony reception of the stranger.

"Leave the room, Rebecca," he said, sharply, "leave the room. May heaven preserve me from such a religious confessor as you."

"I will do as you wish, brother. Madam, I am sorry you have refused to join with me in holy prayer."

Lady Rebecca bowed low. Her salutation was returned by the strange lady, and the former left the room.

"Forgive her," said the earl; "her heart has been frozen by fanaticism. I will summon a servant who will lead you to a chamber. No—no. You cannot—shall not return to the village at this late hour. To-morrow, at daybreak, I shall be stirring, and will send for you to your room if you will kindly meet me so early."

A servant, in obedience to the earl's summons, entered, and led the earl's sister-in-law to her chamber.

CHAPTER XVIII.

"Who ever is the mother of one chylde,
Which having thought long dead she fyndes alive,
Let her by proofe of that which she hath fylde
In her own breast, this mother's joy descrive;
For other none such passion can contrive
In perfect forme, as this good ladye felt,
When she so fair a daughter saw survive."

THE FAERIE QUEENE.

"*Macduff.* O horror! horror! horror! Tongue nor
          heart
Cannot conceive, nor name thee!"

MACBETH.

IN the morning the strange lady was nowhere to be found; her room was
empty, but on the table was discovered a
note addressed to the earl.

He opened it hastily when it was given
him, and read the words—

" My Lord,—

"I cannot stay longer. It is useless. I shall not start for France until to-
morrow. Wherever I go I will correspond
with you regularly. Another interview will
only recall those feelings of remorse and
sorrow we both experienced last night.

"I wish you God's protection.

"ANNETTE."

"She is in the village. I must be off at
once. Fetch my horse. Tell Stephen to
be ready immediately."

"He has not been at the Hall all night,
my lord."

"Then call Ralph."

The man stood shuffling his feet.

"Call Ralph, I say," thundered the earl.

"He hasn't been here all night, my lord."

"What! What does all this mean?"

On further inquiries he discovered that
Ralph and Stephen had left on horseback
in the afternoon of the previous day, and

had not since been heard of. The earl then went to the stable himself, and ordered one of the helpers to saddle his horse. He rode to the village and made inquiries as to any stranger who had been there lately. He found she had been staying at the little inn, but had left some two hours before.

" She has gone on to the coast," he thought.

He rode along the Dover road, making inquiries at every house he passed, and of every one he met, but could meet with no trace of the fugitive. It was late in the day when he returned to the Hall, vexed and disheartened with the fruitlessness of his search.

At the evening meal Ralph's absence was the subject of much speculation. Lady Rebecca was greatly alarmed, and even the earl himself seemed very much concerned about his nephew's disappearance.

" Some strange fatality seems to have befallen the house," said Lady Rebecca. "The first disturbance of our serene repose was the appearance of that strolling girl. Can Ralph have discovered that she is at Lady Claire St. Hiliare's ?"

"He can have no idea where she is," said the earl. "And if he had gone there he would certainly not have taken Stephen with him."

Lady Rebecca made no reply, but sat in her usual posture, rigidly upright, looking into the burning logs upon the hearth. The earl was looking sorrowfully at the lamp, tracing in its flame many scenes that until now had long since laid asleep in the deep recesses of his memory, but had been disturbed and brought to the surface by the appearance of Annette on the previous evening.

At this moment the door opened, and Ralph entered the great hall.

He rapidly walked to the earl, and taking

his hand, exclaimed, in a voice full of joy—

"Uncle, uncle! I have good news—good news. You remember Isabelle—Isabelle, who was at Lady Claire St. Hiliare's—"

"What?" asked the earl and his sister in a breath.

"She awaits you in the outer hall."

"Oh Ralph! Ralph!" said Lady Rebecca, in solemn tones, "what curse are you bringing upon our house?"

"Stop—stop—my dear aunt—"

"Stop! Can my tongue lie still when—"

"It will lie still soon, aunt, in amazement. Isabelle is my cousin—Isabelle is my uncle's daughter."

"Impossible!" exclaimed the earl, his face changing to the hue of death.

"It is true. I have loved her since I first saw her. I traced her to Lady Claire St. Hiliare's. She was wickedly sent away by that woman, and ultimately reached the

forest of Epping, where she and Louisa
stayed. I saw her there. You may frown,
my dear aunt, but you will find that Isabelle is your niece. To make the story
short, I rescued her from imminent peril,
and with Stephen took her to a cottage for
shelter. To this cottage Providence guided
us. It could be only His hand that led us
to that spot, for in that house we found her
old nurse Margaret—"

"Margaret! I remember Margaret!"
gasped the earl.

"She is outside, with sufficient proof to
convince even my aunt yonder that Isabelle
is your daughter."

"Where is she? Where are they?"

Ralph hurriedly left the great hall, and
immediately afterwards returned, leading
Isabelle by the hand, followed closely by
Margaret.

Isabelle looked much refreshed by her
long rest. Her golden hair fell in clusters

over her shoulders, and her blue eyes were raised with a curious, half timid, half anxious look towards the earl.

Old Margaret suddenly came to the front, and looking steadfastly at the earl, exclaimed, "That is the gentleman who came to see your mother the last time I saw her, Miss Isabelle."

"Margaret!" cried the earl, "I remember you. Thank God for this. But this dear girl's mother was not my wife. You remember there were two sisters."

"I remember," said the old woman, "two sisters, the picture of each other— Annette and Alice."

"One was poisoned," said the earl, sorrowfully.

"One was poisoned," responded Margaret, "by a wicked woman; but I call heaven to witness I knew nothing of it—"

"I know it—I know it. The poisoner mistook the sister. The heartless wretch intended to have destroyed Annette. Annette was the—"

"My child! my child!" shrieked a voice from behind the astonished group. Every face turned to see, and beheld the strange lady madly rushing towards Isabelle. Isabelle started, as indeed did all the group.

"Margaret!" exclaimed Annette.

"A spirit! My mistress!" cried Margaret.

The long-thought-dead mother clasped Isabelle in her arms, passionately kissing her, and both sobbing tears of gratitude and joy.

"You are astonished to see me," said Annette, after a little while, and looking towards the earl. "I left, last night, with the intention of never seeing you again, but a strange feeling has been in my breast all day. Some invisible power impelled me here. It is God's holy work. He has moved me to my child. Oh, Isabelle, Isabelle, my own dear daughter—so beautiful —where is the one who has so tenderly nursed you all these years ? God is indeed good. Oh, my heart will burst with gladness. Let me thank—"

A shrill bugle call stopped her voice, and startled every one. Ralph moved instinctively to the side of Isabelle, and taking her hand, grasped it affectionately. In return her soft blue eyes, diffused with tears of joy, looked up into his face with such a sweet expression of love and tenderness, that a flush of delight overspread his features.

"You love my child," said Annette, abruptly, but in a kind, sweet voice. "Are you a Draconbury ?"

"I am the earl's nephew, madam," said Ralph, bowing.

"That voice ! It is the same voice I heard one still night from the lake at Sir Gilbert's house—"

17—2

"Sir Gilbert's house.   Were you—"

A commotion stopped their conversation.

Ralph looked up and saw a tall hand-some man striding up the centre of the hall. His bearing was haughty, but his face beamed with a kind, although some-what sad expression.

"I come to seek the healing of an old feud with an old friend," said the stranger. "I did not stop to be announced. Being benighted in this forest, I thought to ask shelter at this house."

He paused, and looking at the earl, who had bowed meekly and reverentially to the stranger, he said—

"Once the Earl of Draconbury loved Charles Stuart."

Annette had stared at the stranger from the first, like one bereft of sense.

The tall cavalier, too, when he saw her, made one step forward, and with eyes filled with wonder and awe, looked at the lady.

"Charles!" she cried. "It is. Do you know me?"

"Annette! Is it possible! Alive! Then I have been cruelly deceived! I was told you were dead! Ah! I see it all! That dress! Imprisoned! and by the Earl of Draconbury! God's death!" shouted the king, drawing his long rapier, and wheeling quickly round to the spot where the earl stood. "Draw! Coward! Traitor! Double-dyed villain! Draw—mongrel—cur—reptile!"

"No — no — for God's sake, stay!" screamed Annette. "One moment will explain all. He is good and generous. I have been imprisoned, but not by him. I was never in this house till—"

"My gracious liege," said Lady Rebecca, stepping forward, and kneeling at the king's feet, "this lady first came here last night. She has been imprisoned for years, by one Sir Gilbert—"

"Arise, madam, arise," said the impetuous king. "Let no one kneel to me. Enough —enough. My lord, I give you my hand, and in this grasp let all our old friendship— the friendship, Thomas, of our boyhood— let it return and exist between us for ever. But now let me hear. Oh, Annette, why did you leave so—without even saying where I could find my child?"

"She is there!" said Annette.

"Most gracious sovereign," said the earl, "this dear girl is your daughter."

"God have mercy on me," said the king, placing his hand over his heart, and leaning on the table for support. "Come hither, child. Come hither."

All eyes were directed to Isabelle. Her face was pale as death with emotion. Her large blue eyes were gazing at the king in astonishment and awe. She seemed spell-bound for the moment, and then appeared to take one step forward, when, uttering a sharp cry of pain, she fell on the floor ; at the same time the report of a pistol resounded through the hall.

"Hell and damnation !" shouted the king, " is this place accursed ? Who is it ? What ho ! guards ! secure every door— seize every caitiff near the place. Help ! help ! My girl ! my girl ! She is dying !"

The scene which followed was one of terrible confusion. On the floor lay poor little Isabelle, a red stream of life-blood flowing from a small wound in her breast. Her long golden hair fell upon the floor, its ends imbued with the ebbing flood of life. Her large blue eyes, late so bright with the light of her pure young soul, were already fixed with the glassy film of death.

" Ralph ! Ralph !" she gasped.

Half frantic with terror, Ralph had rushed towards the window through which the shot had been fired, shouting, " The dwarf! the dwarf!" but immediately after-

wards returned to the spot where Isabelle
lay, and kneeling down beside her, clasped
her hand, and kissed her pale lips.

She made a faint effort to smile. Ralph,
weeping like a child, bowed his ear closer
to her lips. He heard the words—

"Good bye!"

Her hand then convulsively squeezed his,
and giving one long, deep-drawn sigh, her
young spirit passed to a better world.

CHAPTER XIX.

"The windows of the wayside inn
    Gleamed red with firelight through the leaves
    Of woodbine, hanging from the eaves,
    Their crimson curtains rent and thin.
    As ancient is this hostelry
    As any in the land may be,
        *   *   *   *   *
    Now somewhat fallen to decay,
    With weather-stains upon the wall,
    And stairways worn, and crazy doors,
    And creaking and uneven floors,
    And chimneys huge, and tiled, and tall."
                        TALES OF A WAYSIDE INN.

THE Old Friar Inn stood on the road-
    side between Eltham and Lee. It
was a quaint old house, built long before
the time of Henry the Eighth. Indeed
tradition said that he had, when Maying at

Shooter's Hill, taken shelter there, and tasted its cool foaming ale.

The picturesque old building was encircled by venerable elms, which stretched out their knotty arms around and over the building, as though to shield it from the inclemency of the weather. The wintry wind moaned through the naked branches of the trees, sounding like the low wailings of an Æolian harp; then a sharp gust would come and change the dull funereal wail into a shrill whistle—each branch and twig giving its peal as though the gaunt old trees were for the moment inhabited by a legion of satyrs busy in the production of their wild weird revelries.

The bar window of the Old Friar was gleaming with light, which shone out cheerily into the dark night, and cast a broad bright flood of light across the road, and into the wood beyond.

Within, a roaring fire on the hearth sent

its bright ruddy rays around, lighting up
the features of three individuals who sat
basking in its genial heat. The flickering
light threw on the walls and ceiling their
strange, grotesque, and ever varying sha-
dows, which, as the flames increased or
diminished in brightness, quivered and
danced in the most fantastic manner. The
bright tin and copper utensils hanging
about the walls reflected the blaze, and
were so many trembling, restless points of
light themselves. A sturdy barrel of ale
resting on its side, on a tressle, in the corner, and a few bottles of spirits, constituted
the stock-in-trade of the Old Friar.

" Well, they're a onlucky family," said
the landlord, John Dacon, blowing a cloud
of smoke from his mouth, and looking
affectionately at the clumsily constructed
wooden pipe he held in his hand.

" Some say it was his wife," said Abram
Tenby, the headborough of Eltham, " but

I met the figure that night, and if ever I saw a spirit I believed I saw one then. However, as it has turned out, it proves to have been a human being. But the king was there, too, they say. After many years' quarrel with the earl, he had come to make it up."

"Nay, nay, Abe," said the landlord, "the king came to fight the earl, but this strange lady stopped 'em. See how *apropos* it was."

"What, the fighting?"

"No, fool-man—her being there, or else there 'ud have been a fine to do between the king and the earl."

"But who shot the young lady? That's what I should like to know. They say young Sir Ralph is almost beside himself, and the king was more cut up than he has ever been all his life."

"It must have been a miracle for his heart to have been affected."

"That's almost treason, John. But remember a laughing face and a light, rollicking manner often covers the heart that feels the deepest."

"You are right," said Mrs. Dacon.

"Well, perhaps you are right," said her husband; " but why should the king be so affected?"

"Well, all I know is he was cut up. The servants say he kissed the corpse many times, and actually shed tears over the face of the dead, and then went away sorrowful and mournful to his palace at Whitehall. Poor girl! as sweet and pretty a creature as ever walked—an angel. Ah, man! the king has a kind heart; he is a human being, not a monster of iron, like your Cromwell."

"Cromwell, sir, I say, was a severe——"

"Mussy on us men, don't drag up Cromwell. Don't, for goodness' sake, begin banging at one another about Cromwell. The pair of ye jaw, and jabber, and wrangle till

ye're black in the face, and all about nothing
as concerns the pair of ye. If ye'd lost
your best copper skillet through a jade of a
gipsy, ye might have summat to bicker and
brawl about."

"I hear they're going to bury the poor
girl to-morrow," said John, after he had, by
a peculiar and well-understood look, inti-
mated to his wife that she need not trouble
to continue her observations.

"Yes, to-morrow, John. It will be a
grand sight—at least—God forgive me for
saying so—I mean, a melancholy sight—for
all the maidens of the village are to follow.
Lady Rebecca is going to superintend.
Have you heard of Tony Tilpenden finding
that dwarf upon the river?"

"What dwarf?"

"You haven't heard, then?"

"No," said John, reluctantly, for he felt
annoyed to find that Abe was before him in
the possession of the latest village news.

Abe, on the other hand, was proud of his being in the position of conveying the news first to the " Old Friar Inn," and was not going to communicate the intelligence without being first properly invited to do so.

" What is it ?" asked the landlady.

" What was that, then, friend Abe ?" said the landlord, finding that the headborough wanted a little coaxing.

Abe, looking ponderously important, with great deliberation drank some more ale, blew his nose, and shifted himself in his seat, then looking straight into the fire, he exclaimed—

" Well, it's this—and, if true, it shows that this young Sir Ralph is as cruel and cold-blooded as his father and ancestors have been kind and generous. Tony Tilpenden the other night was cut on the river attending to his nets, when he heard a lot of shrieking, and saw through the darkness,

coming along, a boat. The shrieks came
from this boat, and as Heaven would have
it, the boat came bump against Tony's boat,
and as luck would have it, that was a good
job, for it was half full of water, and in it
lay this poor devil of a dwarf bound hand
and foot."

"Well?" said John.

"Well," continued Abe, "to make a long
story short, Tony pulled him into his boat,
and after a while the poor wretch told his
tale. It seems that this young Sir Ralph
has been trying to get hold of his sister,
and so to get this dwarf out of the way,
he had him put in the boat with a hole
in it, bound hand and foot. Well, the
water of course kept coming in at the hole,
and in a very little time it would have gone
down. The poor wretch of a dwarf was
half dead with fright; besides, he had got
an ugly wound in the shoulder, and Tony
had all——"

At this moment there was a knock at the door.

"Come in," shouted the landlord.

The latch was lifted and a traveller entered. As he, with diffident and faltering step, approached the group so that the full light of the fire fell upon his features, he became an object of interest to the company. His face was pale and haggard, but his eyes were bright, and darted about in restless activity at the three faces before him, and then around the room. His hair was snowy white, and fell down in neglected locks upon his shoulders.

He took a chair offered by the landlady.

"You are travelling late to-night," said the landlord.

"Well, it is not late, nor is it early," said the stranger, with a curious short laugh. "Nothing is late or early to me. It is all the same time—at least—humph—there it is again—such a strange flutter in my head.

I cannot think when I wish to—whereabouts am I? What town, I mean."

"Close to Eltham, master."

"Eltham," he said, looking into the fire and silently watching the flame.

John Dacon turned to his friend, and significantly tapped his forehead with his finger.

"Have you travelled far, master?" asked the landlord.

"Well, it seems a good long way, but I don't know when I began—my daughter— no—it takes two grains of gold—does Margaret live here?"

"Who is Margaret, old man?"

"Why, how you forget. She lived with me—but how long ago was that? Ah, there it is again, that ticking in my head! They put me in gaol."

"Where?"

"Oh, somewhere; but I got out again. Ah! ah! they thought I was old and

powerless, and so they didn't take much
trouble with me, but I outdid them. I
have got a brain—sharp—but it isn't what
it used to be."

" But why did they put you in prison ?"

" One drachm of the pure oil—no, stop—
the two—where am I ?"

" Give him some ale, mother," said the
landlord, in an under-tone, " the poor old
fellow is a little crazy."

Merlin rambled on unheeded by his companions, who soon resumed their conversation respecting the late events up at the Hall.

The old man at first took little notice of
what they said, but gradually his attention
was arrested. He listened apparently with
feverish interest to their discussion, and
after some time he suddenly arose.

" What's the matter, master ?" asked
the landlady, who had all the while looked
upon his movements, and listened to his
mutterings with fear.

"I am going," he answered.

"Where?"

"I don't go anywhere. I am always going, that is all I know. I do not want to go anywhere, but I always go."

"It's a shame," said the landlord, "to let the poor old fellow go out this cold, bleak night. Let's keep him here, Polly. He can sleep in the back room, sure."

"Nay, John, I'll ne'er have a half-crazed fellow in my house. Maybe he 'ud set the house a fire for the fun of it. He has been talking of strange things, and using foreign names as I never heerd before. I believe he is one of them devil-dealing spirit men who worry the stars to let 'em work evil."

"The stars," said Merlin. "Do you know the stars?"

"No, sir, I don't," said the landlady, with a courtesy, for she had a wholesome dread of her strange visitor.

"The stars—ah—the stars," he said,

meditatively, twisting his fingers strangely, and then drawing his forefinger across his brow; "the stars—yes—the stars," he repeated. He lifted the latch of the door, and walked out into the dark, gloomy night.

The three arose simultaneously, and went to the door to watch the figure of the old man disappear in the darkness.

Merlin wandered on muttering to himself. His unseated reason was powerless to guide his steps. In the deep gloom and stillness of the night he wandered along beneath the tall bare trees that rose up on each side of the narrow road.

"What did they mean?" he muttered. "A dead girl with golden hair and blue eyes—just like Isabelle—and the earl—the strange lady—what do they mean—who are all these?"

He wandered on and on—his rambling hesitating footsteps being as uncertain, wayward, and inconsequent, as the thoughts which flew about in his clouded brain.

After some time he saw a large house with lights shining from the windows.

"That is too big," he muttered, stopping to count the windows. "One, two, three, four, five — ah, dozens and dozens — no, perhaps one dozen—lights and windows— that's too large. Margaret and I lived in a smaller house with two windows and a thatch. And Isabelle — no, Isabelle can never be there."

Yet he went on, and entered the grounds of the house. He followed the broad gravel path which led to the front hall. In passing a window he stopped to look in. It was the great hall. He looked in and fancied he remembered the massive fire-place, and the rich oak carving over and round it; the ceiling and the groined roof.

"I have been here," he said, strangely ing his forehead with his hand, " or is

it a place I have seen in a dream? But I
don't remember Isabelle here. Stay. Ah
my thoughts—my will—my power—my
brain fails me—such a fluttering always."

He walked on until he came to the hall
door. He tapped gently at the door. He
stood some time, but the door still remained closed. Again he tapped. It was
opened by a retainer.

"My child—Isabelle?" said Merlin in a
tone of interrogation.

The man had often heard Isabelle's name,
and stepped aside, half divining that the
white-haired old man was he of whom he
had heard so much of late.

Merlin, finding his way unimpeded,
walked in, and with slow and silent step,
turned into the great hall. He paused as
he entered to view the scene before him.
At the far end was a raised bier covered
with white satin, the folds reaching to the
round. On this rested a coffin. Around

on the bier were large wax candles, which cast about and upon the face of the dead a soft rich light. From where Merlin stood he could see the pale clay-like features of the sleeper in death, but he was too far off to trace in their form a resemblance to any one he had known. He stood like one entranced, when his staring eyes, even at that distance, discerned the abundant glossy golden hair —the only thing in death that retains its living aspect.

His agitation was so great that he scarcely had power to move towards the object, which to him seemed to possess such a mystic power of fascination. Slowly at last he walked forward. When he approached the side of the bier he saw the sweet placid face of Isabelle, frozen in the iron grip of cruel relentless death. Those fond laughter-loving eyes were closed for ever—hid beneath the wax-like lids. The mouth, even in death, retained a smile of happiness—a smile that might have been thrown over it by the pure young spirit as it saw, when released from its beautiful yet earthly prison, the glorious realms of the eternal heavens.

Her glossy hair fell in short sprays over her marble temples, and by the side of her wax-like cheeks, and reached far down upon her snow-white breast, across which her little hands rested, folded in calm repose.

Merlin looked at the sleeper in death, and as he gazed a doubt came across his hazy brain. Could she really be dead? So life-like! Could this be death? Was it not merely a deep sleep? He half fancied he saw the white linen, which partly covered her fair bosom, rise and fall as though obeying the regular breathings of the sleeper. But the coffin!

Merlin, clutching his breast with both hands, as though to subdue the wild pulsations of his heart, and thrusting forward his terror-stricken face, as he stared again and again at the face of the dead, exclaimed : "Dead ! no ! She sleeps—it's only sleep !"

"It's death !" said a solemn voice.

Merlin started, and looked up. Not far from the bier sat Ralph. His face was haggard and pale, and filled with the furrows of intense grief. He looked an old man. Four days appeared to have been to him half a lifetime. For, as the rising and setting of the sun had registered the flight of time, it was only four days since he had rescued Isabelle from the barn at Ongar, yet as time had dealt with him, he had lived twenty years in that short period.

"She cannot be dead !" shrieked Merlin.

Ralph made no answer. He believed the figure by the side of the coffin was Merlin. But the events of the last few days had benumbed his reason. He cared for little. He buried his face in his hands, and swaying to and fro moaned aloud. Merlin bent over the coffin. He put forth his hand. It trembled as though he were suffering from ague.

" Isabelle ! Isabelle !" he cried in his most tender accents, as though he would wake her, yet fearing to wake her too suddenly. " Isabelle ! Isabelle !"

He bowed his head, as though he would listen for the breathing. He placed his finger on her cheek, and the icy coldness told him she was dead. Clasping his hands high above his head and looking upward, he shrieked in a paroxysm of grief: " My God ! My God !" and fell lifeless to the ground.

CHAPTER XX.

" Othello. It is the cause, it is the cause, my soul,—
Let me not name it to you, you chaste stars !—
It is the cause :—Yet I'll not shed her blood ;
Nor scar that whiter skin of hers than snow,
And smooth as monumental alabaster.
Yet she must die, else she'll betray more men."
OTHELLO.

THERE was a commotion in the palace yard at Whitehall. The Earl of Draconbury's coach was drawn up on one side, while he and Ralph had just alighted from their horses.

"This way, my lord," said a gentleman-in-waiting.

They were introduced to the king's private apartment. Charles was sitting at a table, alone. His favourite spaniels were at his feet. His brow was contracted, and an expression of sadness was visible in his face.

"Welcome, my lord," said the king, taking the earl's proffered hand, " be seated. I am tired of these fellows. Clarendon has been here with a long tedious story about the state of the navy, and has been talking to me of ships and stores, guns and matchlocks, and a host of other sea-like gear, as though my father had been a purser and my mother a sea-cook. God's life, Draconbury, I don't know how you have been, but since the dreadful event of that awful night I have been oppressed with gloom. I cannot shake it off. Your face, too, betrays that you have suffered much."

"The strange and sudden re-appearance of poor Annette recalled so vividly all that passed years ago—so distinctly—that it seems but yesterday that I went to that room, and found poor Alice dead—poisoned —and my grief has returned."

"Your nephew, poor fellow," said the king, "has terribly altered. Poor Isabelle's death seems to have added twenty years to his life. Cheer up, my young friend. Your life is young yet. Your sorrow is deep, and I can feel for you. My boy, I cannot restore the lost sunshine of your life, but you shall have what you choose—a regiment —or, Mr. Secretary Pepys shall find you a ship to command."

"I thank your gracious majesty for this kindness," said Ralph, in a sad tone. "I stay in England for one purpose only—to destroy the wretch who shot poor Isabelle. After that I leave this country for ever."

"Nay. We cannot lose thee. Time will alter your plans. Time, the only killer of grief, will make you think again of my offer. Alas! that my little daughter should be snatched from me just as I had found her after all those years. These

strange unaccountable things tempt one
to disbelieve in a Ruling Power."

"We must submit to God's will, sire,"
said the earl. "Our knowledge is limited.
We cannot presume to penetrate the wisdom
of His decrees."

"I know, I know, my lord," said the
king. "Say no more. Say no more."

He buried his face in his hands, and,
resting his elbows on the table, remained
silent for some moments. Then, as though
with an effort, he aroused himself, and exclaimed—

"You have done as I wished with her
remains ?"

"Your majesty's wishes have been fulfilled to the letter."

"Take care of Annette."

"She has expressed her determination
not to dwell in the Hall, but I think she
is inclined to remain near the resting-place
of Isabelle. I thought of building a cot-

tage in the plantation, or wherever she might select."

"A good thought, Draconbury. I was coming to see her, but I have been so pestered with these ministers."

"She is in my coach outside. She insisted upon coming ever since she saw this letter—"

"What letter?"

"One of my people found in the grounds a letter which I think points to where we may hear something of the wretch who fired the fatal shot."

"Where is it? Who is it? By heaven he shall die!"

The earl handed a letter to the king, who read as follows :—

"To Master Zermat.

"As far as I am concerned, the existence or death of the girl you call little

Isabelle, is a matter of indifference. All I
wish is, that she may be kept from the sight
of the king. I thought you wished to
marry her. I am engaged now, and cannot
see you, so I write this letter. Call in a
few days, as I wish you to give me as
faithful a picture of the doings in the in-
terior of the palace, as it seems you gave
to Merlin of my chamber. You will understand me. I have done my part of the
compact—now I shall expect you to do
yours.

"CLAIRE."

"Claire!" said the king, dropping the
letter on the floor, and speaking in the
most sad and melancholy tones. "Claire!
the woman I have loved so fondly—the only
heart I thought I could trust, the only soul
I thought pure and true. Oh, humanity!
humanity! The longer I live the less I
see to admire and respect, and the more I

find to detest and abhor. After this sting
from the woman I have loved above all
others I believe in nothing—I believe in
no one."

He sat silently brooding for some moments, and then exclaimed—"But how is
it she knew anything of Isabelle? Can you
explain?"

The earl then related how Isabelle had
been found by him in the forest—her resi-
dence at his house—the cause of his taking
her to Hamil House, and her sudden disappearance therefrom, adding—

"But before your majesty censures me
for thus dealing with one of royal blood,
remember that I was ignorant of her
parentage—remember, sire, that had I
known or dreamt who she was, no fond
father would have been more careful of her
welfare than I."

"1 know it—I know it."

"From that letter your majesty will see

we may probably hear something of this dwarf at Hamil House."

" We must go there at once."

" Annette is with us. She insists upon seeing Lady Claire."

" Why ?"

" Heaven only knows. Directly she saw the writing she was terribly affected, and insisted upon coming with us."

" That is strange. You say she is below."

" She is in the coach."

" I will go at once to this Hamil House."

He summoned an attendant.

" Tell Garston to follow me immediately, with a company of halberdiers."

In less than ten minutes from that time the king, the earl, and Ralph, left the gate of the Palace yard, followed by Annette in the coach.

Behind followed the soldiers, according to the king's orders.

19—2

CHAPTER XXI.

" *Cæsar.*   Poison'd then.

*   *   *   *   *

Most probable,
That so she died; for her physician tells me,
She hath pursued conclusions infinite
Of easy ways to die."

ANTONY AND CLEOPATRA.

WHEN the cavalcade arrived within sight of Hamil House, the king called the colonel to his side.

"Garston," he said, "I am going to visit that house yonder. When I enter, surround the grounds, and see that no one passes out. I shall take a dozen of your men with me. I shall walk straight into the room I wish to visit, without being announced. In order to accomplish this, I shall seize every servant that appears. You understand?"

"I understand your majesty. I should be more at ease, however, if it had so pleased your majesty to arrange that I could accompany you, and leave a subordinate in command of the troop outside."

"Well you can do that, Garston, if you wish."

The king, and the earl, and Ralph, then dismounted, and Annette was handed from the coach.

In answer to a knock at the gate the Spaniard appeared, and was instantly seized and bound by the troopers.

The colonel, with twelve men, then passed through the gate, followed by the king and his party.

They entered the great hall. An unfortunate retainer hearing the clatter, came from the back offices of the house to ascertain the cause. He was instantly seized and bound, and sent to the troopers at the gate and placed under guard.

The king led the way to Lady Claire's private room, where he believed he should find her. He remembered the way he had gone when disguised as an Asiatic. When they arrived at the door he turned and said—

"Now we have reached so far there is little fear of any opposition within here. It is my wish," he said, addressing the earl and Ralph, "to enter first. Afterwards, at a signal, you can also come in."

"We have much pleasure in obeying your majesty's commands," said the earl; "but is it policy to risk your life alone?"

"There can be no risk," responded the king.

"There may be, sire."

At this moment Annette stepped forward
and exclaimed—

"Your majesty must let me accompany
you."

"You, Annette!"

"Yes, sire. You will see that I have good
reason to ask this favour. Nay, I demand it."

"Demand!" said Charles with a slight
frown, but it soon passed away.

"My appearance will paralyze the writer
of that letter, sire."

"There is more in this than I can
fathom," said the king.

"There is, and I pray you, Charles, let
me accompany you. Let us enter at once,
for I am burning with impatience."

"Well—as you wish," he said, as he
turned the handle of the door and entered
with Annette.

At the table sat Lady Claire, and opposite her sat the dwarf. At a little distance
behind stood Josephine.

"This sudden intrusion!" said Lady Claire, half in anger, half in astonishment,. "and with a lady——"

She stopped, for her face turned deadly pale. Her eyes seemed starting from beneath the lids; her teeth became clenched; and her features were convulsed with an expression of dread, agony, and horror.

"My lady—my lady, what is it?" screamed Josephine, rushing towards her mistress. "It is only the king, madam, and some one else."

"Some—one—else!" said Lady Claire, in a deep sepulchral tone. "It is a spirit! Can the dead then rise again? Why do you haunt me?"

The king stared with amazement at the effect produced upon Lady Claire by the appearance of Annette.

He looked at Annette for an explanation.

Annette walked slowly towards the table. As she advanced step by step the dread and terror of Lady Claire seemed to increase. Her lips were pale as death; they moved as though she attempted to speak, but no sound came from them. She trembled as though with an ague, till the table on which her hands rested for support vibrated visibly; yet all this while her eyes were fixed upon the approaching figure which seemed to inspire her with so much horror.

"That face," said Annette, advancing, "it is the same face. It is fifteen years since, but those features and the events of that terrible day were burnt into my memory by the sight of the swollen and disfigured face of my poisoned sister."

Lady Claire shrieked and sank into a chair.

"What is all this?" said the king, looking from one to the other.

"Call in the Earl of Draconbury," said Annette.

The earl and Ralph entered.

"That woman," said Annette, looking at the earl, and pointing towards Lady Claire, "that woman, with that fair face, is the woman who poisoned your wife."

"What!" gasped the earl. "Lady Claire St. Hiliare!"

"It is a lie—it is a lie!" screamed the accused woman, jumping to her feet, her eyes flashing with pride and indignation, for she knew it was her last throw for the king's love, for power, for fame, for happiness, nay, perhaps for existence—she knew it was the last time those fascinating features would ever serve her, and into her expressive face she threw every art, every emotion, that could either work upon the human passions and sympathies of the men present, or evince the scorn and indignation of an innocent and injured heart. "It is a lie!" she repeated, firmly. "Who are you?"

"Who am I?" said Annette, in a sad

quiet voice, so strangely in contrast to the passionate tone of Lady Claire. " I think you recognized me long before I spoke. I think his majesty observed your terror. Your face, madam, was pallid with fear —with dread of the dead ! Your face, madam, reflected the horror of your wicked soul ! Your face, madam, showed that you recognised in me one who is the image of your victim."

" How could you be my victim when you are still alive ?"

" A clear admission, I think, my lord," said Annette, looking towards the Earl of Draconbury.

" Damnable phantasy, what mean you ?" said Lady Claire. " Is this some trick ? Yet that face !"

" Aye, yet that face, madam. I repeat your words to show how they incriminate you. I will draw a picture. Do you remember a small room in Paris,

with two windows that looked on to the
Seine—"

Lady Claire shuddered.

"I see it touches a tender chord of
memory. Do you remember a bed on which
lay a young mother? A woman visited
that room, and, pretending she had mistaken
the apartments, left, but she did not leave
until she had exhibited a strong sympathy
for the weak mother, and poured into her
drink what she called an Eastern liquid
balm—that balm was poison."

"Liar!"

"That woman was you. Do you remember the face of your victim? Look at
mine!" said Annette, staring steadfastly at
the accused woman.

Lady Claire gasped. Her features worked
convulsively. Even her long tried and
well practised facial powers were unable to
prevent the terror of her soul from flashing
into her countenance. She sank on the

chair and appeared as though about to swoon, but again making a superhuman effort, she arose, and placing her hand on the table to steady her quivering frame, she exclaimed—

"Who are you? I know nothing of what you say! I cannot understand any of this."

"But how terribly agitated you seem at what you do not understand," said Annette, with biting sarcasm.

"Will your majesty—will Lord Draconbury—am I to be insulted in this manner, ill as I am suddenly smitten—I am unwell, very unwell to-day—I have been ill all day, and your majesty should not have thus burst in upon my privacy, especially with this adventuress—this cruel liar. What! you believe— ?"

She stopped, for the cold looks of the king, and the earl, and Ralph, plainly denoted their sympathy was with the accuser.

"Woman!" said Annette, "murderess! you poisoned my sister. My Lord Draconbury, this is the creature who destroyed your wife. That is why I wished to come here."

"Do you know this letter, madam?" said the king, sternly, walking towards her ladyship.

"What! Charles!" said Lady Claire, throwing into her interesting face a most sweet expression of love—a winning smile which she had known many times before to have turned his anger into affection. "What, Charles! are you to be an accuser also?"

"Your smiles are useless, madam. I have loved you I candidly confess, but I little believed beneath that fair face was a heart that must have been made in hell."

"Oh, Charles! Charles!"

"Read that, madam. Read!" shouted

the king, in anger, thrusting into her hand the fatal letter.

Lady Claire looked at it. It fell from her hand. Her head dropped.

"All is lost!" she muttered.

"Lost! yes!" roared Charles, in a paroxysm of rage; and striking the table with his sword, he shattered it in two. "Do you know that Isabelle was my daughter?"

"My God! my God! Mercy!" said Lady Claire.

"Mercy!" said the king, contemptuously, "seize her."

No one stirred. The tremendous passion of the king dismayed every one. He walked to the window and appeared to be endeavouring to allay his anger.

Suddenly Lady Claire arose. Again she seemed to have miraculously summoned from some hidden resource renewed vital energy.

She with her arm pushed Josephine on
one side, and, looking defiantly at the
group, for they were staring with astonishment at the extraordinary fluctuations in
the physical power of the wonderful creature before them, she exclaimed :

" Poison !   Well, I did poison your wife,
my Lord of Draconbury, but I thought she
was the king's mistress.   Charles," she said,
turning to the king, "as I have loved you
above all the world, even better than myself, so now I hate you with the same intensity.   It is for this that I have lost
name, respect, and all sense of honour and
virtue, to please your base love, and this is
your return.   If the curses of a woman can
affect your despicable nature, may you ever
be miserable.   Accursed be the day that I
ever came to dwell amidst this white-livered
race, whose very king is a poltroon and a
coward.   I will show you the spirit of a
woman of Seville.   Your cold, pale-faced

dames of the north, here, can suffer and live. They cling to life as a worm would. A curse on your daughter. I hated her blue eyes and golden hair when I first saw her here, as only one woman knows how to hate another. You think to try me by jury—your boasted English fashion—to make me a spectacle for a gaping crowd. I defy you. Curse you. Curse you all— heaven—hell—the universe! Farewell!"

Before the king, or Josephine, who seemed alone to divine her intentions, could seize her hand, she had taken from her bosom a small substance and, placing it on her tongue, swallowed it.

As they seized her empty hand she gave a sickly laugh—a laugh denoting in its sar- castic sound derision for those around her, yet there was something appalling in the hysterical sob which followed, showing the dread she felt of the dark eternity into which she was plunging.

She still stood by the table, supporting herself by her hands resting upon it. She still looked around at the group with a fiendish cunning expression. They all viewed her with horror. Presently her face became flushed; her cheeks became swollen, and her lips were purple. Her eyeballs were terribly dilated with a horrible expression. Those features lately so beautiful, were transformed into the face of a demon. Her breath became heavy and short. Rapidly her face, neck, bosom, and hands, assumed a black hue, and in a few moments she fell on the floor a corpse.

"God Almighty save us," said the king, rushing from the apartment, followed by all—even Josephine joining them in her anxiety to get from the horrible black thing that lay swollen on the floor.

"Here is one prisoner," said Colonel Garston, as they reached the outside of the door.

It was the dwarf. He had attempted to escape from the room when the king first entered.

"Take him away," said the king. "He murdered one I love deeply. After that need I tell you my wish?"

"No, sire," said the colonel.

The dwarf was bound and marched away from the house under the guard of the troopers.

Out in the fields of Marylebone, away from the noise and bustle of the City, a file of soldiers were preparing for the death of a prisoner. That prisoner was Zermat.

He was placed at a distance of six paces from the firing squad. His miserable supplications for mercy, and yells of despair, filled the soldiers with disgust. On finding his death was inevitable he threw himself on the ground, shrieking and yelling in the most horrible manner, and writhing and

20—2

bounding about in such a way that the men were unable to take proper aim.

" Bind the wretch to a tree," shouted the officer.

Zermat was then taken, still uttering the most abject appeals for mercy, strangely intermingled with frightful and blasphemous imprecations upon those around him, and bound to a tree with his face towards the firing party.

" Fire !" cried the officer.

There was a sharp cracking of reports, a blaze, and a cloud of smoke ; when this had rolled slowly away the dwarf's head was seen to be hanging on his breast, pierced by a dozen bullets.

THE END.

BILLING, PRINTER, GUILDFORD.